Teaching NIGHT

**Created to accompany
the memoir by Elie Wiesel**

FACING
HISTORY
AND
OURSELVES

Facing History and Ourselves is an international educational and professional development organization whose mission is to engage students of diverse backgrounds in an examination of racism, prejudice, and antisemitism in order to promote the development of a more humane and informed citizenry. By studying the historical development of the Holocaust and other examples of genocide, students make the essential connection between history and the moral choices they confront in their own lives. For more information about Facing History and Ourselves, please visit our website at www.facinghistory.org.

Copyright © 2017 by Facing History and Ourselves, Inc. All rights reserved.

Facing History and Ourselves® is a trademark registered in the US Patent & Trademark Office.

ISBN: 978-1-940457-23-9

CONTENTS

Using This Study Guide — 1
Exploring the Central Question — 1
Section Elements — 2
Supporting the Memoir with Historical Context — 2
Helping Students Process Emotionally Powerful Material — 3

Section 1 Pre-Reading: The Individual and Society — 5
Overview — 5
Introducing the Central Question — 5
Activities for Deeper Understanding — 6
Map: Eliezer's Forced Journey — 9
Reading: Elie Wiesel's Childhood — 10
Visual Essay: Pre-War Sighet — 12

Section 2 Introducing NIGHT — 21
Overview — 21
Exploring the Text — 22
Connecting to Central Question — 22
Activities for Deeper Understanding — 22
Handout: Identity Timeline — 24
Reading: The Holocaust in Hungary — 25
Handout: Iceberg Diagram — 27
Reading: The Difference between Knowing and Believing — 28

Section 3 Separation and Deportation — 31
Overview — 31
Exploring the Text — 31
Connecting to the Central Question — 32
Activities for Deeper Understanding — 32
Reading: Universe of Obligation — 37
Handout: Universe of Obligation — 39
Reading: Witnesses, Bystanders, and Beneficiaries in Hungary — 40
Handout: Night and Day — 42
Handout: Found Poem: Mrs. Schächter's Vision — 43

Section 4 Auschwitz-Birkenau — 45
Overview — 45
Exploring the Text — 45
Connecting to the Central Question — 46

Activities for Deeper Understanding	47
Visual Essay: The Auschwitz Album	50
Reading: Auschwitz	56
Reading: A Commandant's View	58
Reading: Voices from Auschwitz: Charlotte Delbo	60

Section 5 Moral Complexity — 63

Overview	63
Exploring the Text	63
Connecting to the Central Question	64
Activities for Deeper Understanding	64
Reading: Choiceless Choices	67
Reading: The Role of the Kapo	68
Reading: Varieties of Resistance	69

Section 6 Faith and Survival — 71

Overview	71
Exploring the Text	71
Connecting to the Central Question	72
Activities for Deeper Understanding	73
Reading: Faith after the Holocaust	76
Reading: Quotations about Michelangelo's and Bak's Work	78
Image: Creation of War Time, *Samuel Bak*	79
Image: Creation of Adam, *Michelangelo*	80

Section 7 Final Days — 81

Overview	81
Exploring the Text	81
Connecting to the Central Question	83
Activities for Deeper Understanding	83
Reading: Forced March	86
Reading: After Liberation	87

Section 8 Post-Reading: Memory and Responsibility — 89

Overview	89
Activities for Deeper Understanding	90
Reading: Forgetting Isn't Healing	92
Reading: The Holocaust as Call to Conscience	94

NIGHT Glossary Terms — 95

USING THIS STUDY GUIDE

Note on edition: This study guide is based on the 2006 edition of *Night*, translated by Marion Wiesel and published by Hill and Wang, a division of Farrar, Straus and Giroux, New York.

> **Teaching strategies, videos, and media referenced throughout this guide can be found at hstry.is/TeachingNight.**

Night is a terse, terrifying account of the childhood experiences of Elie Wiesel during the Holocaust. As a testimony of immense suffering from one of the darkest moments of history, *Night* requires readers to confront the worst of what humans are able to do to each other. As a work of literature, Wiesel's memoir also asks students to explore the ability and, especially, the limitations of language to convey human experience.

This resource is designed to guide teachers and students through an experience of *Night* that engages the mind, heart, and conscience. This approach will develop students' literacy skills, promote their historical understanding of the Holocaust, and foster empathy, perspective taking, and other social-emotional skills. Most importantly, the goal of this guide is to facilitate a reading of *Night* that helps to sensitize students to inhumanity and suffering and to encourage them to make choices that help to alleviate, rather than to perpetuate, those experiences in the world around them.

Exploring the Central Question

A primary through line in *Night*, and in this guide, is the theme of identity and how it is influenced by society and the circumstances of our lives. The central question below is designed to connect classroom discussion and activities to this larger theme.

Q: *How is our identity shaped and reshaped by the circumstances we encounter? How do tragedy and trauma influence an individual's identity and choices?*

Within the broad theme of the relationship between the individual and society, the central question focuses students' attention on the identity of Eliezer, the name Wiesel goes by in the memoir, as it is shaped and challenged by the searing events of the Holocaust. Though Wiesel's story is singular, these questions also invite students to consider the relationship between identity, time, and place in their own lives.

The central question is introduced in Section 1 and is revisited regularly in subsequent sections. By returning to the central question at regular intervals, students will be able to trace how their thinking has developed and deepened over the course of their study of the memoir. The discussion questions and activities throughout this guide also support students' exploration of the central question.

Section Elements

This resource is organized into eight sections. In addition to supplying pre- and post-reading activities, the guide is designed to support the careful reading of specific pages of the memoir. Each section is broken into three main components:

- **Exploring the Text:** primarily text-based questions designed to deepen students' understanding of the memoir, including Wiesel's use of language and literary devices, and to prompt reflection on its themes. You can use these—and your own—questions as journal or discussion prompts to guide students' exploration of the text.

- **Connecting to the Central Question:** a repeating prompt for students to connect what they have learned from activities and analysis in each section to the larger theme of identity in the memoir. By returning to the central question in each section of the novel, students will be able to trace how their thinking has developed and deepened over the course of their study of *Night*.

- **Activities for Deeper Understanding:** suggestions for writing, reflection, and discussion-based activities that support literary analysis and introduce important historical context for the events that take place in the memoir. When appropriate, these activities also invite students to make thematic connections between *Night* and other texts and universal human behaviors. Choose from these activities to find those that best suit your learning goals and the needs of your students.

While it is crucial that students have the opportunity to respond to *Night* both intellectually and emotionally, the extent to which teachers engage their students in the activities in this guide that extend beyond the pages of the memoir itself will vary depending on available class time and the support students need in understanding the text.

Supporting the Memoir with Historical Context

At the time Wiesel's story begins, most of what we now understand as the Holocaust had already happened. Much of *Night* takes place within a single year, 1944–1945. In this short time, and in Wiesel's compressed writing style, the story unfolds from the perspective of Eliezer. As readers engrossed in Eliezer's painful story, we often share his uncertainty and confusion about the events that will transform his life. In the early pages of the memoir, Wiesel makes passing references to the progress of the war and the political context, but because we are hearing the story largely from Eliezer's point of view, the broader historical context is never fully explained. Many questions may surface for students: What are the Germans doing in Sighet? Who is fighting the war, and why? Why are the Jews being targeted for deportation and death?

Offering some answers to these questions, and introducing the history of ideas, events, and decisions that shaped the world of Wiesel's memoir, is an essential part of teaching *Night* and a core component of this guide. This history includes the ideology of anti-Judaism and antisemitism, the rise of the Nazis in Germany in the 1920s and 1930s, and the evolving persecution and murder of Jews and other targets throughout Europe. If it's true, as philosopher José Ortega y Gasset observes, that "I am myself and my circumstances,"[1] then these events are the "circumstances" students must grasp in order to understand Eliezer and his story.

You will find a wide range of primary and secondary sources woven throughout the sections of this guide, designed to help students develop a nuanced understanding of this complex and disturbing period of history so that they can place the memoir and its meaning in a larger, more universal context.

Helping Students Process Emotionally Powerful Material

From the very beginning of *Night*, Elie Wiesel introduces stories and images that are emotionally troubling and even graphic. The deeply personal and emotional events of *Night* can help to foster engagement and empathy in students, yet they can also be disturbing. Before you begin to teach the book, it's important to acknowledge that students may have a range of emotional reactions to this challenging text. Some students may respond with sadness, anger, or disgust, while others may not find the story powerful to the same degree. In addition, different people demonstrate emotion in different ways. Some students will be silent. Some may laugh. Some may not want to talk. Some may take days to process difficult stories.

We urge teachers to create space for students to have a range of reactions and emotions as they read, and to establish practices in the classroom to reflect on this emotionally powerful material. Below are three strategies that you can use repeatedly during your teaching of the memoir.

1. **Exit Cards**: Exit cards ask students to briefly respond to a question on a small piece of paper, like an index card, and hand it in before leaving class for the day. These cards offer immediate feedback for teachers about what students are thinking and feeling in response to a lesson or activity. One simple prompt for an exit card is, "What questions, ideas, and feelings did today's class raise for you?"

2. **Journals**: Journals provide a safe, accessible space for students to share thoughts, feelings, and uncertainties as they work with difficult material. They foster a practice of reflection and document students' evolving thinking. Journal writing can be used as homework to prepare for class discussion; it can also bring valuable moments of silence into the classroom. Any kind of notebook can be used for a journal; what is important is that a student's journal entries are collected together.

   There are many different ways to focus students' writing in journals. The following are a few approaches that work well with *Night*:

   - **Sentence stems:** "This section of the memoir makes me feel . . ."; "As I read this section of the memoir, I wondered . . ."; "If I could talk with one of the characters in the memoir, I would want to say/I would want to ask . . ."

[1] José Ortega y Gasset, *Obras Completas*, Vol. I (Madrid: Taurus/Fundación José Ortega y Gasset, 2004), 757.

- **Lifted line responses:** Students select a particular quotation that strikes them and then answer such questions as, "What is interesting to you about this quotation? What does it make you think about? What questions does it raise for you?"
- **Freewriting:** Students use a defined amount of time to write in silence about any aspect of their reading that is on their mind.

3. Color, Symbol, Image: This strategy invites students to reflect on ideas in non-verbal ways and encourages them to think metaphorically. Students first focus on something they've just read and think about the most important theme, idea, or emotion that surfaced for them. Then they reflect on how they can communicate the essence of what they've read using a color, a symbol, and an image.

SECTION 1

Pre-Reading:
THE INDIVIDUAL AND SOCIETY

Overview

Although it reads like a novel, *Night* is a memoir. Wiesel described it as "an autobiographical story, a kind of testimony of one witness speaking of his own life, his own death."[1] The term *memoir* comes from a Latin word meaning "to remember," and in his book, Elie Wiesel recalls what he saw and experienced during the period from 1941 to 1945. From a deeply personal perspective, he shares how his experiences transformed his identity and sense of self. This pre-reading section therefore focuses on the relationship between the individual and society, linking young Eliezer's evolving identity with the context of the place where he grew up and, later, with the traumatic events of the Holocaust that so profoundly shaped his life. It also invites students to consider the relationship between identity, time, and place in their own lives.

To provide context for what students are about to read, the suggested activities in this section offer insight into Wiesel's life before the war and help students to imagine his community in Sighet before it was uprooted and destroyed. This section also offers resources to help students understand the historical context of Nazism and the Holocaust, including ideas, people, and events that shaped Wiesel's experiences but are only briefly mentioned in his memoir.

Introducing the Central Question

Like all memoirs, *Night* invites readers to reflect on the theme of identity. The central question that will guide students' reading of *Night* addresses this theme:

Q: *How is our identity shaped and reshaped by the circumstances we encounter? How do tragedy and trauma influence an individual's identity and choices?*

Before introducing this central question to the class, it will be helpful to hold an initial discussion about the concept of identity. Our identity is a combination of many factors. It includes the words and phrases we use to describe ourselves and the labels others place on us. Gender, ethnicity, religion, occupation, and physical characteristics are all part of one's identity. So are ties to a particular neighborhood, school, or nation; our values and beliefs; and the events that have shaped our lives. Identities are rarely truly fixed or settled; they are constantly shifting in response to our environment and experiences.

---

[1] From Henry James Cargas, *Conversation with Elie Wiesel* (Justice Books, 1992), 86.

Begin a discussion about identity by sharing philosopher José Ortega y Gasset's observation: "I am myself and my circumstances."[2] Ask students to respond to the following prompts, either independently in their journals or in small groups using the Big Paper teaching strategy:

- How could you paraphrase Ortega y Gasset's words?
- What do you think he means by "circumstances"?
- What is he trying to say about where identity comes from?
- Is there a time when his observation has been true in your own experience?

Discuss students' responses as a group, and then share the central question with students. Discuss as a class: How do your reflections on Ortega y Gasset's words help you to form an initial response to the central question?

Activities for Deeper Understanding

1. Introduce Eliezer and His Community

Explain that students will be reading and discussing an autobiographical story of a young boy's experiences in Europe during World War II and the Holocaust. That boy's life didn't begin and end with the war: he had an identity, a family life, and a community, just as students themselves do.

Introduce students to Wiesel's life before the memoir begins through primary sources. If you haven't already, you may want to share copies of the glossary on pages 95–99 before students begin reading.

- The reading Elie Wiesel's Childhood introduces aspects of his life before the events of *Night*. Students can use this reading to begin to gather ideas about young Eliezer's identity (for example, they could represent his identity before the war visually using the Identity Charts teaching strategy), as a prelude to examining the way that external and internal conflicts transform him over the course of the memoir they are about to read. If you think your students will find this reading challenging, you may want to use the Chunking teaching strategy.

- Just like Elie Wiesel himself, his hometown of Sighet had its own identity and culture. Located in the Carpathian Mountains of the Transylvania region, Sighet was part of Romania following World War I; later it changed hands and was part of Hungary from 1940 to 1944. The town was a predominantly Jewish community before it was irrevocably changed by the war and the Holocaust. Yet images of individuals and the community survived.

    As you begin to read *Night*, locate Sighet on the map Eliezer's Forced Journey. As the class progresses through *Night*, they can find other important locations in Eliezer's story on this map.

    After locating Sighet, explore the Pre-War Sighet visual essay, which includes photographs of Jewish celebrations, families, and daily life, to get a glimpse of Elie Wiesel's world, to anticipate the scenes and characters in the memoir, and to

---

[2] José Ortega y *Gasset, Obras Completas*, Vol. I (Madrid: Taurus/Fundación José Ortega y Gasset, 2004), 757.

reflect on the gravity of what was lost. Students can also view this collection of photographs at hstry.is/TeachingNight, or you can copy and display them in the classroom.

Use a simple critical viewing teaching strategy called See, Think, Wonder to help students engage with the images. As students view each photograph, ask them:

- What do you see? What details stand out? (At this stage, elicit observations, not interpretations.)
- What do you think is going on in this image? What makes you say that?
- What does this photograph make you wonder? What broader questions does it raise for you?

If students have explored the reading Elie Wiesel's Childhood, ask them how they might connect the photographs in the visual essay with the people and places that Wiesel has described in words. Ask: How do these images extend your thinking about Elie Wiesel's identity? Later, as you begin reading *Night*, you could return to these images to ask similar questions.

2. Explore the Historical Context of Night

Our multimedia timeline, Historical Context for Night (see hstry.is/TeachingNight), features mini-documentary films as well as primary source readings and eyewitness accounts of the years preceding *Night*. The timeline can be accessed directly by students, or you can select and assign just a few elements as part of your lesson. Together, these resources help students understand both the broad history and the difficult choices faced by individuals and groups in the years before Wiesel's account begins.

Below are three different approaches to bringing the historical context for *Night* into your classroom using the interactive timeline.

a. **Build basic historical knowledge with a flipped classroom approach:** Assign students to watch a selection of the mini-documentary films for homework, and ask them to capture the most important events depicted in those films. In class, work together to build a timeline for 1918–1945.

b. **Connect the broad sweep of history with decisions made by individuals and groups:** In class, watch the mini-documentary Step by Step: Phases of the Holocaust (see hstry.is/TeachingNight). Then discuss the following:

- What events does Bergen reference?
- How does she define the phases of the Holocaust?

Follow the film with a selection of readings, drawn from the interactive timeline, that take students deeper into the dynamics and decisions of each phase. (The connection questions that accompany each reading can be used as journal or in-class discussion prompts to deepen students' comprehension and reflection.)

Afterward, discuss as a class: How do these readings help us to understand choices that led to the Nazi rise to power in Germany, the targeting and persecution of Jews, and the death of millions in the Holocaust?

c. **Make a human timeline:** The Human Timeline teaching strategy uses movement to help students understand and remember the chronology of events. Students can work with the interactive timeline as the central text for this activity. By combining, deleting, or adding events, you can adapt the interactive timeline to best meet the needs of your students.

Once you have assigned events to students (individually or in pairs), they can use the associated mini-documentaries or readings and make notes to share with their classmates when they present their events as part of the human timeline.

As students present their events, ask others to discuss these questions: What might be some of the causes and consequences of this event? How does this event relate to those that came before and after it?

Eliezer's Forced Journey

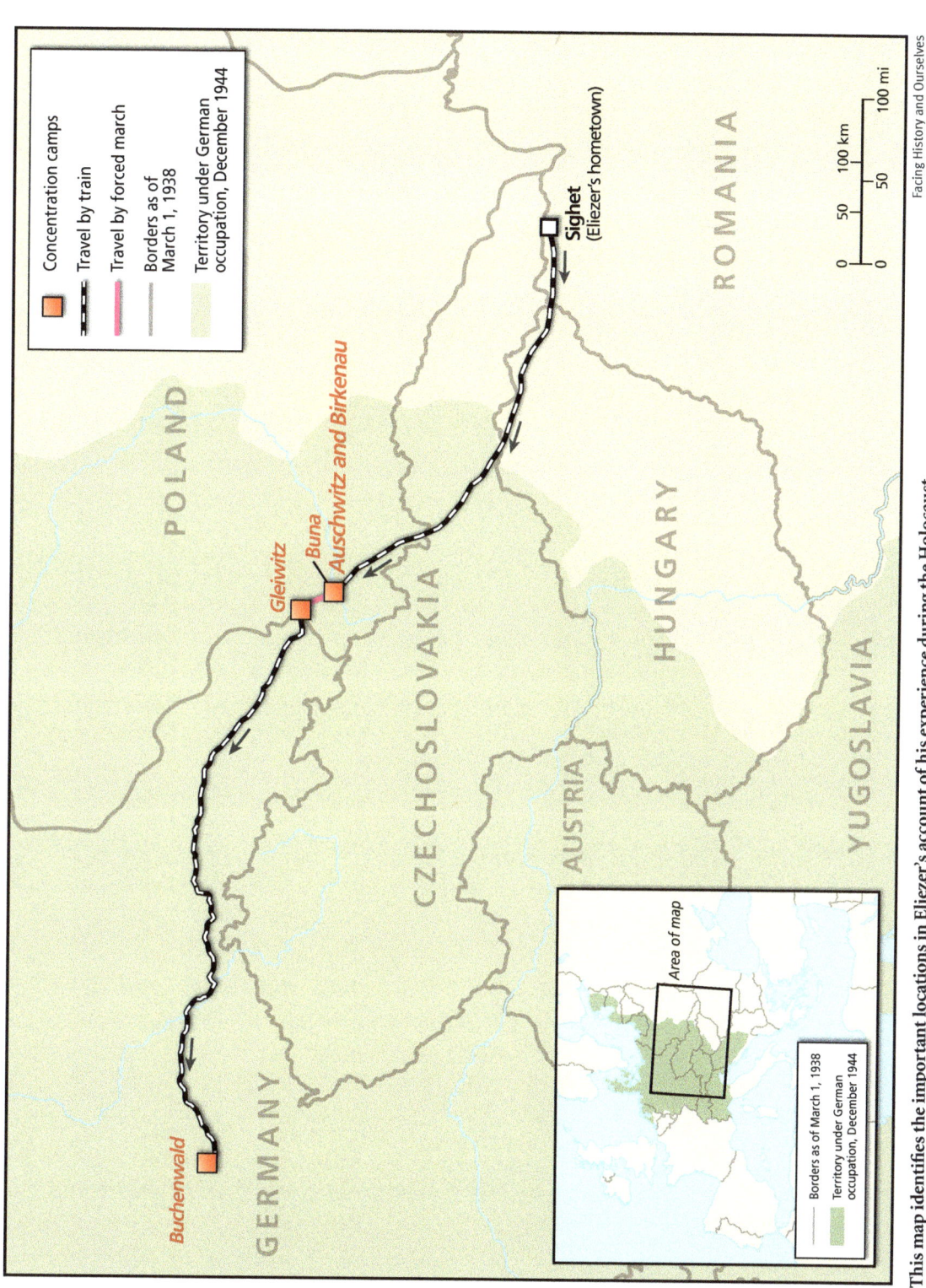

This map identifies the important locations in Eliezer's account of his experience during the Holocaust.

Elie Wiesel's Childhood

Elie Wiesel was born in 1928 in Sighet, a border town that changed hands between Romania and Hungary several times during his life. Sighet was a community with a significant population of observant Jews, like Wiesel's family. Wiesel introduces Sighet in the early pages of *Night* but tells readers much more about his early life there, his family, and his faith in a later memoir called *All Rivers Run to the Sea*:

> Shabbat (the Sabbath) was the only day I spent with [my father]. In Sighet, Shabbat began on Friday afternoon. Shops closed well before sundown, stragglers and late-comers having been admonished by rabbinical emissaries and inspectors: "Let's go, it's late, time to close up! Shabbat is coming!" And woe to him who disobeyed. After the ritual bath we would walk to services, dressed for the occasion. Sometimes my father would take my hand to protect me, as we passed the nearby police station or the central prison on the main square. I liked it when he did that, and I like to remember it now. I felt reassured, content. Bound to me, he belonged to me. We formed a bloc. . . .
>
> Friday was our special time. I would stop and see [Grandma Nissel, his paternal grandmother] on my way home from *heder* [Jewish school]. "Eliezer, my boy, come, I'm waiting for you!" she would call out from her window. She would give me fresh buns from the oven and sit and watch fondly, her hands folded, happy and at peace, a glimmer in her blue-gray eyes, as I washed and recited the appropriate prayer. . . . I would look at her as I ate and, fifteen minutes later, I would get up. "I have to go home and get ready, Grandma. Shabbat will be here any minute now." But then, when I was already at the door, she would call me back. "Tell me what you learned this week." It was part of our ritual. I should share a Bible story or, later, an insight of the Midrash (commentary on the Bible text). . . .
>
> [S]tudy became a true adventure for me. My first teacher, the Batizer Rebbe, a sweet old man with a snow-white beard that devoured his face, pointed to the twenty-two holy letters of the Hebrew alphabet and said, "Here, children, are the beginning and the end of all things. Thousands upon thousands of works have been written and will be written with these letters. Look at them and study them with love, for they will be your links to life. And to eternity."
>
> When I read the first word aloud—*Bereshit*, "in the beginning"—I felt transported into an enchanted universe. An intense joy gripped me when I came to understand the first verse. "It was with the twenty-two letters of the *aleph-bet* (Hebrew alphabet) that God created the world," said the teacher, who on reflection was probably not so old. "Take care of them and they will take care of you. They will go with you everywhere. They will make you laugh and cry. Or rather, they will cry when you cry and laugh when you laugh, and if you are worthy of it, they will allow you into hidden sanctuaries where all becomes . . . " All becomes what? Dust? Truth? Life? It was a sentence he never finished.
>
> There was something terrifying and fascinating about reading ancient texts, something that filled me with awe. Without moving I could ramble through worlds visible and invisible. I was in two places at once, a thousand places at once. I was with Adam at the beginning barely awakened to a world streaming with light; with Moses in Sinai under a flaming sky.[1]

---

1   Elie Wiesel, *All Rivers Run to the Sea: Memoirs* (New York: Alfred P. Knopf, 1994), 4, 6, 10–11.

Connection Questions

1. What in Elie Wiesel's life sounds familiar or unfamiliar to you? What questions do you have? When you remember your childhood, what things come to mind about your traditions? How are they similar to or different from what Wiesel remembers?

2. Based on the reading, what do we know about Wiesel's/Eliezer's identity—his family, his religion, his culture, his values, and more?

3. What quotations are most revealing about who he is?

Pre-War Sighet

Students at Kheyder

Students sitting at a traditional Jewish religious school, or kheyder, in 1920s Sighet.

YIVO Institute for Jewish Research

Sighet before World War II

An image of the main market square in the Transylvanian town of Sighet, Romania, taken before World War II.

Members of Sighet's Jewish Community

A group photo in front of Sighet's synagogue, ca. 1930–1939.

United States Holocaust Memorial Museum, courtesy of Mitchell Eisen

Leaders of Sighet's Jewish Community

Leaders of the Jewish community in Sighet, including Mr. Hershkovich, Mr. Klein, Mr. Yacobovich, and Mr. Jahan, ca. 1928–1930.

Yosef Meir Weiss

Portrait of Yosef Meir Weiss, the Spinka rebbe from Sighet, 1906.

Sighet Soccer Club

Members of Sighet's Samson Soccer Club, ca. 1930.

Weaving Workshop at a Yeshiva

Students in a weaving workshop at a yeshiva, or rabbinical academy, in Sighet before the war.

YIVO Institute for Jewish Research

Pre-War Jewish Family

A Jewish family, possibly in Sighet, taken before the beginning of World War II, ca. 1930–1940.

United States Holocaust Memorial Museum, courtesy of Solange Dratler Lebowitz

Wiesel Family

A young Elie Wiesel with his mother and sister before World War II.

SECTION 2

INTRODUCING *NIGHT*

Reading Assignment

Pages 3 – top of 10

Overview

Night begins in 1941 in Sighet, Hungary. Author Elie Wiesel tells the story from the point of view of his younger self, called Eliezer, who is almost 13 years old when the book begins. Eliezer introduces readers to his family, his community, and to a daily life dominated by religious faith, study, and ritual observance. Young Eliezer is desperate to study Kabbalah, a type of Jewish mysticism, and becomes close to Moishe the Beadle, an impoverished man who tutors him in this spiritual practice.

Soon, all foreign Jews are expelled from Sighet, including Moishe. He and the others are shipped to German-occupied Poland, where the Nazis force them to dig their own graves before slaughtering them. Moishe miraculously escapes, and in 1942 he returns to Sighet to alert his friends to the danger, but no one believes him. Throughout 1943, life in Sighet goes on as usual, and Moishe grows more silent and withdrawn. By the spring of 1944, the townspeople are hopeful that the war will soon be over. They hear on the radio that Russian troops are advancing farther and farther west. But within days of those broadcasts, German soldiers appear on the streets of Sighet.

We encourage teachers to provide ample time for discussion after reading this section, and to use some of the strategies for processing emotionally powerful material described on page 3.

Exploring the Text

Ask students for their questions or comments about what they have read in this section. Then use the following questions as journal or discussion prompts to guide students' exploration of the text.

1. What do we learn about Eliezer's identity from the opening pages of the memoir? What does he value? What does he hope for? What troubles him? (If students have read Elie Wiesel's Childhood, on page 10, they can also compare Wiesel's portrayal of his young self in these two texts.)

2. What role does Moishe the Beadle play in Eliezer's life?

3. How does Eliezer view Moishe at the beginning of the book? How do others in Sighet regard Moishe? How do those views change over the course of this section of the book?

4. What did Moishe witness when he was shipped to Poland? Why does he want the Jews of Sighet to know what he saw?

5. How do the Jews of Sighet respond to Moishe's stories?

6. What do the Jews of Sighet know about events beyond the town by the spring of 1944? How do you account for the way they respond to what they learn by word of mouth, over the radio, and from their own experiences?

7. Eliezer recalls townspeople hearing news of the Russian front and saying, "Hitler will not be able to harm us, even if he wants to." Eliezer comments, "Yes, we even doubted his resolve to exterminate us" (page 8). What does the language of this passage reveal about Eliezer's point of view? How does the tone of this statement reveal the difference between what the narrator knows and what young Eliezer, the boy in the story, is aware of?

8. Why do you think Elie Wiesel begins *Night* with the story of Moishe the Beadle? What lessons does he seem to learn from Moishe's experiences in telling his own story?

Connecting to the Central Question

After exploring the text and reviewing the events that take place in this section of the book, give students an opportunity to revisit their thinking about this guide's central question:

Q: *How is our identity shaped and reshaped by the circumstances we encounter? How do tragedy and trauma influence an individual's identity and choices?*

Give students a few minutes to reflect and write in their journals about any changes they have noticed in Eliezer at this early stage in the book. If you are having students use identity timelines (see below), these may help with this reflection. Do the students' observations about Eliezer's changing identity support their initial thinking about the central question? Or do they prompt them to revise their thinking?

Activities for Deeper Understanding

1. Create an Identity Timeline

In an identity timeline, students synthesize events in the memoir with quotations that reflect Eliezer's changing identity. Creating such a timeline and adding to it as they move through the memoir helps students to document their observations about Eliezer's identity and to deepen their thinking about the central question. The timeline can also become fodder for class discussions and analytical writing assignments.

Distribute copies of the Identity Timeline handout. (If students gathered information about Eliezer's pre-war identity in Section 1 or created an identity chart for him, they can draw on that information in their first timeline entry.) As the story unfolds, remind students to add more events, words, and quotations to the timeline.

2. Activate Historical Knowledge

In the previous section, students began building knowledge of the historical context of Elie Wiesel's memoir. As Eliezer tells us of life in Sighet in 1941–1944, readers with knowledge of history are aware of what he and his family do not know or choose not to believe: the majority of Jews in German-occupied lands have already been murdered, and the Jews of Hungary are next.

As you read this section of the memoir with students, the following activities can help to activate their historical knowledge:

a. **Build understanding of Hungary's history with text-to-text connections:** This section of *Night* includes many references to Hungarian history. To help students understand this national context, distribute the reading The Holocaust in Hungary and make "text-to-text" connections between this historical reading and Wiesel's memoir. How does the historical text connect to *Night*, extend students' thinking about the memoir, and challenge or complicate students' understanding?

b. **Make an iceberg diagram:** The Iceberg Diagram teaching strategy helps students gain awareness of the multiple causes that give rise to a specific event, like the expulsion of foreign Jews from Sighet, that may seem to happen quite abruptly but is in fact the result of complex forces and longstanding processes. Distribute copies of the Iceberg Diagram handout. Then ask students to brainstorm what gave rise to the expulsion and massacre of Sighet's foreign Jews. Their answers might include Hungarian antisemitism, the rise of the Nazis in Germany, Nazi ideology, German expansionism, and the events of World War II, drawing on students' prior knowledge and on the pre-reading work you did as a class. They should write these causes beneath the surface of the water on the diagram. (You may also want to create iceberg diagrams at other points in the memoir—for example, when Eliezer and his family are deported to Auschwitz.)

c. **Reflect on dramatic irony:** Dramatic irony exists when readers are aware of events or circumstances in a story of which the characters have no knowledge. Ask students to identify one or more moments of dramatic irony in the opening pages of *Night*. What do we as readers know in that moment that characters in the memoir do not? What does the author know that he as a younger person did not, and how does that show in the telling of the story? What effect does this gap between our knowledge and that of the characters have on you as a reader? How does it make you feel?

3. Explore the Difference between Knowing and Believing

Distribute the reading The Difference between Knowing and Believing and use the Connect, Extend, Challenge teaching strategy to help students relate the reading to this section of *Night*. (You may want to return to this teaching strategy as students consider other readings as part of this study guide.)

Connect: How do the ideas and information in this reading connect to Wiesel's memoir?

Extend: How does this reading extend or broaden your thinking about *Night*?

Challenge: Does this reading challenge or complicate your understanding of the memoir? What new questions does it raise for you?

HANDOUT

Identity Timeline

Create an identity timeline for Eliezer. Above the line, write words or phrases that describe Eliezer throughout the memoir. Each word or phrase should be supported with a quotation from the text. Below the line, record key events in the memoir with approximate dates (if possible). The first entry has been added.

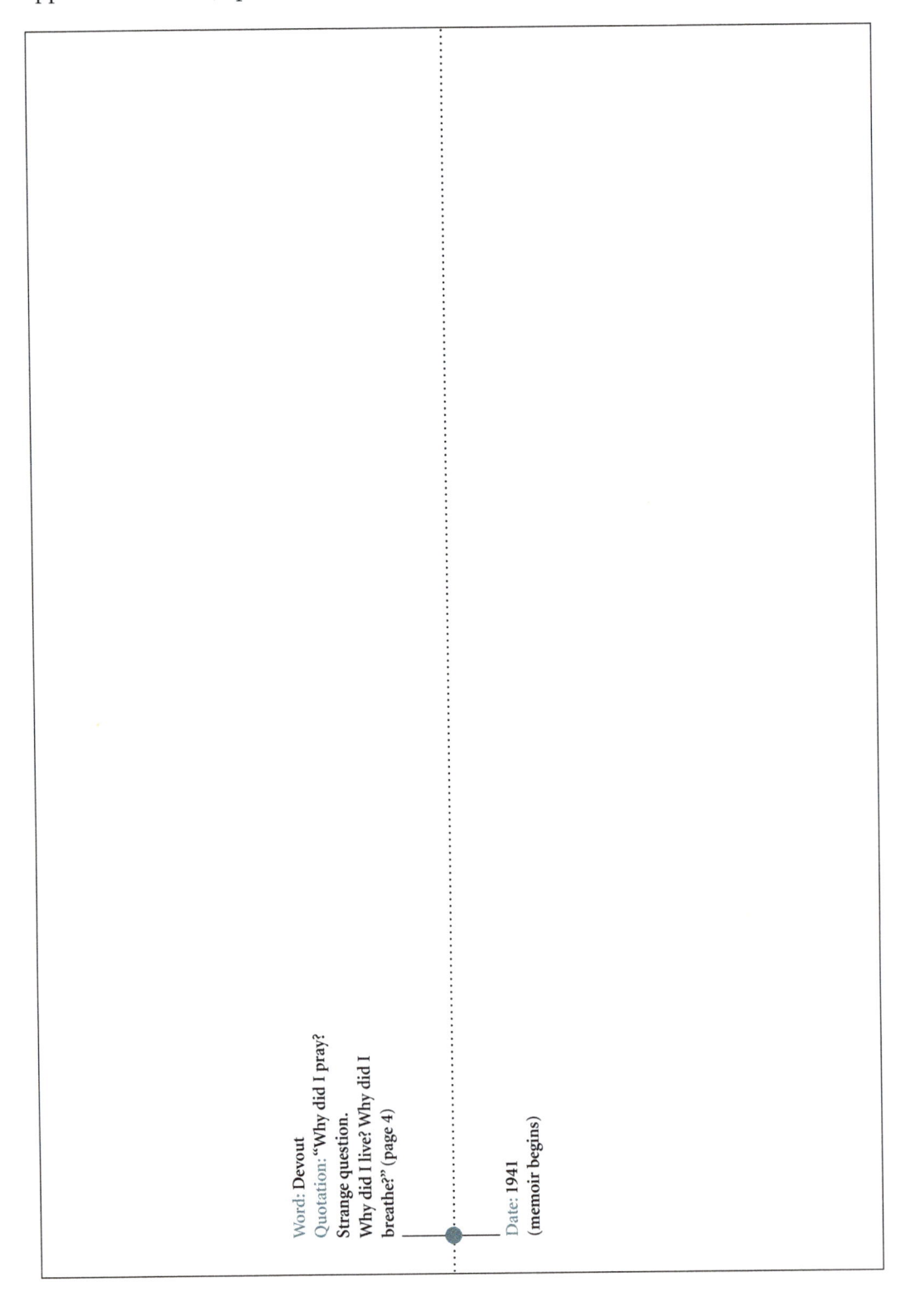

Word: Devout
Quotation: "Why did I pray? Strange question. Why did I live? Why did I breathe?" (page 4)

Date: 1941 (memoir begins)

24 Teaching NIGHT

The Holocaust in Hungary

Much of *Night* takes place within a single year, 1944–1945. It was the final year of what later became known as the Holocaust. Between 1939 and 1945, Adolf Hitler and his followers murdered about one-third of all the Jews in the world (and millions of other civilians), in the midst of the most destructive war in human history. Young and old alike were killed solely because of their ancestry.

The Jewish community in Hungary was large and diverse. Jews had lived in the area for more than a thousand years, and after the Jewish population was granted legal and economic freedoms in the late 1800s, their numbers grew. In the capital, Budapest, where Jews made up more than 20 percent of the residents, they were often professionals who played influential roles in the cultural and intellectual life of the city. Elsewhere in Hungary, Jewish people lived more traditional, rural, and often impoverished lives.

When the Austro-Hungarian Empire collapsed after World War I, Hungary entered a period of unrest. Like Russia, which was transformed by a communist revolution, Hungary had a brief experiment with communism. This experiment came to an end with a counter-revolution called the White Terror. During this period, Jews, who were often stereotypically and inaccurately associated with communism, faced renewed antisemitism. Hungary's conservative leader, Regent Miklós Horthy, defeated the communists, restored order, and enacted laws that restricted the legal and economic rights of Jews. As historian Paul Shapiro points out, "Antisemitism in Hungary did not arrive from abroad."[1]

In the late 1930s, Hungary made an alliance with Nazi Germany. Germany offered the largest market for Hungary's agricultural produce, and, most importantly, Nazi Germany's expansionist goals aligned with Hungary's own ambition to reclaim territories it had lost in World War I. During most of the war, Hungarian Jews suffered discrimination and harassment, but they were largely protected from the Nazis' killing machine. (Hungary's foreign-born Jews were an exception. As Elie Wiesel recounts in *Night* through the story of Moishe the Beadle, in 1941 foreign Jews were rounded up, deported, and used as slave laborers or murdered.) Regent Horthy, despite pressure from right-wing parties and Hitler, refused to deport Hungarian-born Jews to Nazi death camps. Still, even before the German occupation, as many as 60,000 Jews died in antisemitic massacres or as slave workers in the military, fighting alongside the German army even as Germany faced increasing defeats at the hands of Soviet forces.

In 1943, Hitler sensed correctly that the Hungarian government was searching for a way out of the alliance. In fact, by the spring of 1944, Hungarian officials were in secret negotiations with Allied forces for a possible armistice. In response, Germany occupied Hungary, though Horthy was allowed to remain as regent. Hungary, which had lost its army earlier in the war, could offer only minimal resistance.

---

[1] "The Testimony of Paul A. Shapiro, U.S. Holocaust Memorial Museum," March 19, 2013, Hungarian Spectrum website, http://hungarianspectrum.org/2013/03/20/the-testimony-of-paul-a-shapiro-u-s-holocaust-memorial-museum/.

Nazi leader Adolf Eichmann came to Hungary to carry out what Nazis called the "Final Solution"—the murder of Hungary's Jewish population. Historian Paul Shapiro explains,

> [B]etween April and July 1944, over 400,000 Hungarian Jews were driven from their homes, concentrated in ghettos, and deported to Auschwitz, where the overwhelming majority of them were gassed on arrival. It was the Hungarian gendarmerie and police who identified and concentrated the Jews, loaded them onto trains, and delivered them into the hands of German SS units waiting at the German-Hungarian border. This process continued systematically until only the Jews of Budapest remained alive.[2]

Threatened with war crimes by Allied leaders, Regent Horthy ordered the deportations, which were being carried out by Hungarian forces, to cease. He sought an armistice with the Soviet Union, whose troops were close to Hungary. In response, the Germans helped to oust Horthy in a coup. A new government, led by the Hungarian fascist Arrow Cross Party (known as *Nyilas*), took over.

Shapiro continues,

> The weeks that followed saw a combination of forced ghettoization in Budapest; death marches involving men, women and children, whose slightest misstep was rewarded with a bullwhip or a bullet; and renewed deportations to Auschwitz. *Nyilas* gangs engaged in wild shooting orgies in Budapest. They massacred the patients, doctors and nurses at the Maros Street Jewish Hospital, to give just one example, and considered it sport to shoot Jews seized at random into the Danube from the riverbank. Three months of *Nyilas* government cost the lives of an additional 85,000 Hungarian Jews.

> Hungarian collaboration and complicity in the Holocaust was thus substantial, as were the losses suffered by this once-large and great Jewish community. Statistics can speak volumes. Nearly one in ten of the approximately six million Jews murdered in the Holocaust was a Hungarian Jew. One of every three Jews murdered at Auschwitz was a Hungarian Jew . . . Some 28,000 Romani citizens of Hungary were also deported and fell victim to this horrific carnage.[3]

---

2 Ibid.
3 Ibid.

Iceberg Diagram

When people say that something is the "tip of the iceberg," they mean that it is a small, visible part of a much larger and more complex issue, just as the part of an iceberg that is visible above water is much smaller than what lies beneath.

This iceberg represents the expulsion and massacre of Sighet's foreign Jews, which occurs early in *Night*. What are some of the forces that led to this event? Draw on your prior knowledge and the historical context you studied to name some of the events, beliefs, and decisions that led to the death of Sighet's foreign Jews. Write them in the underwater part of the iceberg.

The expulsion and massacre of Sighet's foreign Jews

The Difference between Knowing and Believing

Jan Karski was one of the first people to share eyewitness accounts of ghettos and camps with Allied leaders outside Europe. Karski, a Catholic Pole who had worked for the Polish diplomatic service before the war, was a courier for the Polish resistance. In the fall of 1942, he was ordered to travel to London and give a report on the situation in occupied Poland to Polish government-in-exile leaders and other high-level officials, including the British foreign minister. Afterward, Karski traveled to the United States, where he met with President Franklin Roosevelt. To prepare his report, Karski met secretly with representatives of two large Jewish organizations. He recalled:

> Both men were in despair. They were fully aware that the deportations from the Warsaw ghetto as well as from other ghettos in Poland would lead to the extermination of the Jewish people. . . . They both stressed that unless dramatic, extraordinary measures were immediately put into effect, the entire Jewish people would perish. . . .[1]

The two men also insisted that Karski should see for himself what was happening to Jews, because his own eyewitness account would make his report more convincing.

As a result, before Karski traveled to London and the United States, he was smuggled into and out of the Warsaw ghetto and the Izbica transit camp. But even his firsthand accounts of what he witnessed there were not able to persuade many of the officials he later met:

> It is not true, as sometimes has been written, that I was the first one to present to the West the whole truth of the fate of the Jews in occupied Poland. There were others. . . . The tragedy was that these testimonies were not believed. Not because of ill will, but simply because the facts were beyond the human imagination.
>
> I experienced this myself. When I was in the United States and told [Supreme Court] Justice Felix Frankfurter the story of the Polish Jews, he said, at the end of our conversation, "I cannot believe you." We were with the Polish ambassador to the U.S., Jan Ciechanowski. Hearing the justice's comments, he was indignant. "Lieutenant Karski is on an official mission. My government's authority stands behind him. You cannot say to his face that he is lying." Frankfurter's answer was, "I am not saying that he is lying. I only said that I cannot believe him, and there is a difference."[2]

Among those who dismissed the reports of German atrocities as war propaganda was W. A. Visser 't Hooft, a Dutch theologian and the first secretary of the World Council of Churches. He changed his mind only after hearing an eyewitness account.

> From that moment onward I had no longer any excuse for shutting my mind to information which could find no place in my view of the world and humanity. And this meant I had to do something about it.

---

1 Quoted in Maciej Kozlowski, "The Mission that Failed: A Polish Courier Who Tried to Help the Jews," in *My Brother's Keeper: Recent Polish Debates on the Holocaust,* ed. Antony Polonsky (London: Routledge, 1990), 83.
2 Quoted in ibid., 87–88.

A considerable number of people in Germany, in occupied countries, in the allied and neutral countries heard stories about mass killings. But the information was ineffective because it seemed too improbable.[3]

Visser 't Hooft believed that "people could find no place in their consciousness for such an unimaginable horror and that they did not have the imagination, together with the courage, to face it. It is possible to live in a twilight between knowing and not knowing. It is possible to refuse full realization of facts because one feels unable to face the implications of these facts."

[3] W. A. Visser't Hooft, *Memoirs,* 2nd ed. (London: World Council of Churches, 1987), 166.

SECTION 3

SEPARATION AND DEPORTATION

Reading Assignment

Pages 10–28

Overview

This section of the memoir describes the immediate physical and emotional impact of the German occupation on Elie Wiesel's life. Events unfold at a rapid pace. German officers and Hungarian police force the Jews of Sighet into two ghettos, where they soon learn of their impending deportation. Caught between hope and terror, Eliezer and his family frantically prepare for their journey. A few of their Hungarian neighbors attempt to help them, while most turn their backs.

Despite efforts by Eliezer's father, a pillar of the local Jewish community, the entire Jewish population of Sighet is eventually marched to the railroad station and deported in overcrowded cattle trains, headed to an unknown destination. On the journey from Sighet, Mrs. Schächter, a neighbor of the Wiesels', insists that she sees a fire. No one else can see the fire, and the other people in the cattle car are first disturbed, then outraged, by Mrs. Schächter's screams. When the train finally pulls into a station, the first thing Eliezer sees is flames rising from a tall chimney. They have arrived at the death camp of Auschwitz-Birkenau.

Exploring the Text

Ask students for their questions or comments about what they have read in this section. Then use the following questions as journal or discussion prompts to guide students' exploration of the text.

1. How does the German occupation change Eliezer's life and that of others in Sighet? How do the Jews of Sighet react to the German decrees, the creation of ghettos, and the news of their impending deportation?

2. How does Wiesel portray the mood in Sighet and the attitudes of his family and community? What imagery does he use to describe the transformation in the town and its inhabitants? What other words, phrases, and images convey a sense of tension and contradiction? If you find passages that reveal how Eliezer's sense of self is shifting in response to these events, add them to your identity timeline.

3. Wiesel writes, "The ghetto was ruled by neither German nor Jew; it was ruled by delusion" (page 12). What do you think he means? What other events, characters, and language in this section reflect the "delusion" in Sighet?

Record an event on your identity timeline.

4. As the last convoy of Jews walks through town to the trains, Wiesel describes "our friends of yesterday" watching though their windows (page 22). Who are the "friends of yesterday"? What other examples can you find of how other residents of Sighet respond to the separation and deportation of the town's Jews? (See also Activity 2 below.)

5. Why does Mrs. Schächter scream in the cattle car? Why does she later become silent and withdrawn?

6. How do people in the cattle car react the first time Mrs. Schächter screams? How do they respond when her screams continue?

7. Compare and contrast Moishe the Beadle and Mrs. Schächter. How do people in Sighet react to these characters and explain their behavior? How would you explain it?

8. Why do you think Wiesel tells the story of Mrs. Schächter? What do you think the experience meant to young Eliezer? What role does the story play in the way the adult Elie Wiesel constructs his memoir and foreshadows events to come?

9. In this section of the memoir, Eliezer mentions a number of events that take place for the first time or the last time. What are they? Why do you think Wiesel chose to draw attention to them?

Connecting to the Central Question

After exploring the text and reviewing the events that take place in this section of the book, give students an opportunity to revisit their thinking about this guide's central question:

Q: *How is our identity shaped and reshaped by the circumstances we encounter? How do tragedy and trauma influence an individual's identity and choices?*

Give students a few minutes to reflect and write in their journals about the changes they are noticing in Eliezer's identity as the Germans occupy Hungary and he and his family are deported to Auschwitz. If you are having students use identity timelines, they may help in this reflection. Do the students' observations about Eliezer's changing identity support their previous thinking about the central question? Or do they prompt them to revise their thinking?

> **Refer to your identity timeline.**

Activities for Deeper Understanding

1. Introduce Universe of Obligation

The persecution and violence of Nazi Germany created terrible dilemmas for people living under the control of the Third Reich. In every place where Jews lived, including Sighet, people watched as Jews were marked and identified, displaced from their homes, and confined to ghettos. Sometimes they also witnessed their deportations and even their murder. Some participated in the crimes; others attempted to help; most watched silently.

The choice to participate in persecution, to help victims, or to stand by is often shaped by an individual's "universe of obligation"—the term sociologist Helen Fein coined to describe the circle of individuals and groups within a society "toward whom obligations are owed, to whom rules apply, and whose injuries call for amends."[1] Those within a society's universe of obligation can expect respect and protection; those outside it become vulnerable, not only to being deprived of rights, privileges, and economic benefits but also to expulsion, physical harm, and, in the most extreme cases, genocide. Like societies, individuals have their own universes of obligation. This activity allows students to explore this concept.

Distribute the reading Universe of Obligation. Discuss the connection questions that follow the reading, and then give each student a copy of the Universe of Obligation handout. Give students time to complete the activity sheet.

In groups of two or three, have students discuss the experience and process of thinking through and illustrating their universes of obligation. In their discussions, they should address the following questions:

- What was the experience of defining your universe of obligation like?

- What did you think about when deciding where to place certain groups in your universe of obligation? Which decisions were difficult? Which were easy?

- Under what conditions might your universe of responsibility shift? How might it shift in times of terror?

- What do you think is the difference between an individual's universe of obligation and that of a school, community, or country?

As an extension, students can use the Universe of Obligation handout to create universes of obligation for different individuals and groups in *Night* using evidence from the text, as described in the next activity.

2. Define the Range of Human Behavior

Examining why some people tried to defy the Nazis and aid Jews while so many others, including world leaders and their governments, did not act provides an entry point for exploring the range of human behavior, in this history and beyond. Within that range of human behavior are the roles of *perpetrator, victim, bystander,* and *upstander,* which can be assumed by individuals, groups, or even nations. But it can be difficult to define each term clearly.

For example, under the label *upstander*, we often list those who take a variety of actions, including resistance and rescue. However, upstanders might also include those who are able to maintain a part of their identity despite opposition, such as people who continue to secretly practice their religious faith or those who refuse to give up hope.

The term *bystander* can be even more complicated. In most dictionaries, it means a person who is simply "standing by" or who is present without taking part in what is going on—a passive spectator. But some scholars, like psychologist Ervin Staub, believe that even passive spectators play a crucial role in defining the meaning of events by implicitly approving of the actions of perpetrators. As students read Wiesel's

---

[1] Helen Fein, *Accounting for Genocide* (New York: Free Press, 1979), 4.

memoir, they will be introduced to characters whose actions and choices reflect this full range of human behavior.

   a. Begin this activity by asking students to brainstorm about the four roles identified above, *perpetrator*, *victim*, *bystander*, and *upstander*, working in pairs or small groups to create working definitions for each. Then ask them to look through the pages of *Night* that they have read so far to identify characters and groups whose actions fit each definition, recording their observations in their journals.

   Some of the characters and groups that students can focus on include:

   - Moishe the Beadle
   - Eliezer and his family
   - The Wiesels' former maid, Maria
   - The Hungarian policeman who knocks on the Wiesels' window
   - Members of the Jewish Council
   - Hungarian policemen who manage the deportations (sometimes called the Gendarmerie)
   - Citizens of Sighet
   - German soldiers and Gestapo

   What role or roles best describe each of the characters or groups? Do some of them fit into multiple roles? Does the text offer any clues as to what shaped their attitudes? (If you completed the universe of obligation activity, students can explore how these characters define their sense of obligation.) Did their roles or behavior change from pre-war Sighet to the period of war and occupation? Are there characters or groups whose behavior doesn't fit within one of these roles? If so, encourage students to identify another role (like *collaborator* or *witness*) to describe these characters. Students should cite evidence from the text to support their claims.

   b. Discuss as a class:

   - How did each student group identify the roles played by different characters and groups? Which were more challenging to place? Did students propose other roles or words that better describe the character or groups they focused on?
   - Is there any evidence in the text to explain how people in Sighet became victims, bystanders, perpetrators, and upstanders? How do the historical sources you reviewed in the earlier sections help you to understand their choices?
   - How do you think people in each role defined their universe of obligation? How did people in these various roles impact Eliezer and his family? What are the consequences when a community or nation removes people from its universe of obligation?

   c. You can deepen students' thinking about the choices and impact of bystanders by reading and discussing Witnesses, Bystanders, and Beneficiaries in Hungary and by viewing Marched to the Ghetto (see hstry.is/TeachingNight), Barbara Fishman

Traub's video testimony about her family's experience of being confined and deported from Sighet.

d. Finally, ask students to revise their working definitions for the different roles based on the sources and the class discussion. How did this activity change or complicate their thinking about the range of human behavior and the roles people play? Students can return to their working definitions and use them to analyze the actions of other characters as the memoir unfolds.

> **Note:** It is important to recognize that it is not these labels themselves, as words, that matter; it is the way we think and talk about the actions (or inactions) of others that helps us both understand history and make connections to the choices we all make in the present. In addition, it is important to remember that individuals and groups usually do not fit into only one category. Instead, they may move into and out of these roles throughout their lives. But by studying history with these terms in mind, despite those limitations, we can think about the agency of individuals, groups, and nations—their ability to recognize the options available to them and make choices that impact their own lives, the lives of others, and the course of history.

Read for Meaning: Imagery and Symbolism

Night is a very short book with an outsize impact on readers. Elie Wiesel has described his writing style as "deliberately spare . . . Every phrase was a testament. There was no time or reason for anything superfluous."[2] One key element that gives Wiesel's compressed style such power is his use of symbols—things, places, or people that have a more than literal meaning and stand for something beyond themselves.

As the title of the book and one of its most frequently evoked images, *night* becomes more than just a marker of time: it is a powerful recurring symbol throughout the memoir. Wiesel often draws on other times of day, including "dawn" and "day," to convey mood and meaning.

"Night," "day," and other markers of time will be important throughout the memoir. You can begin a conversation about symbolism by first asking students to brainstorm the possible symbolic meanings of "night" and "day" outside of Wiesel's story. Where have they seen references to "night" and "day" in popular music, in other literature, or in artwork? What did "night" and "day" represent in these contexts?

Next, distribute the Night and Day handout to help students track Wiesel's references to night and day and to reflect on the meaning of each example. Because it's often easier to analyze a symbol after finding several examples, we recommend that students gather a few different examples on their chart before considering the meaning Wiesel gives to different times of day. What do these words suggest in the early pages of the book? How does their meaning change as the story unfolds? What impact do they have on the reader? How does Wiesel use this literary device to animate his story and amplify his message?

---

2 Elie Wiesel, *All Rivers Run to the Sea: Memoirs* (New York: Knopf, 1995), 321.

4. Create Found Poems

One of the most striking scenes in this section of the memoir is Mrs. Schächter's outburst in the cattle car. Filled with tension, foreshadowing, and symbolism, it is an emotionally powerful and unsettling moment. The Found Poems teaching strategy gives students the opportunity to pay close attention to this scene's language, to process its emotions, and to create their own poem that distills the essential themes and meaning of the passage. Distribute the handout Found Poem: Mrs. Schächter's Vision and have students create found poems individually or in pairs or trios.

After students have completed their poems, give them the opportunity to share their work. You can ask each student to read his or her poem to the class, do this in pairs, or divide the class into small groups for sharing.

After students have had the opportunity to hear each other's poems, lead a class discussion. You might choose from questions 5–9 on page 32, as well as the questions below:

- What strikes you about these poems?
- What do they have in common? How are they different?
- What surprised you as you heard them?
- What do you see or understand about this scene after writing and hearing the found poems that you may not have before?
- How did working so closely with this text affect you? What did these words make you think and feel?

Consider asking students to create found poems using other powerful passages from *Night* as they continue reading the memoir.

Universe of Obligation

What does it mean to be a member of a group? In groups we meet our most basic needs; in groups we learn a language and a culture or way of life. In groups we also satisfy our yearning to belong, receive comfort in times of trouble, and find companions who share our dreams, values, and beliefs. Groups also provide security and protection from those who might wish to do us harm. Therefore, how a group defines its membership matters. Belonging can have significant advantages; being excluded can leave a person vulnerable.

How the members of a group, a nation, or a community define who belongs and who does not has a lot to do with how they define their *universe of obligation*. Sociologist Helen Fein coined this phrase to describe the group of individuals within a society "toward whom obligations are owed, to whom rules apply, and whose injuries call for amends."[1] In other words, a society's universe of obligation includes those people who that society believes deserve respect and whose rights it believes are worthy of protection.

A society's universe of obligation can change. Individuals and groups that are respected and protected members of a society at one time may find themselves outside of the universe of obligation when circumstances are different—such as during a war or economic depression. Beliefs and attitudes that are widely shared among members of a society may also affect the way that society defines its universe of obligation. For instance, throughout history, beliefs and attitudes about religion, gender, and race have helped to determine which people a society protects and which people it does not.

Although Fein uses the term to describe the way nations determine membership, we might also refer to an individual's universe of obligation to describe the circle of other individuals that person feels a responsibility to care for and protect. Rabbi Jonathan Sacks describes how individuals often define those for whom they feel responsible:

> [Eighteenth-century philosopher] David Hume noted that our sense of empathy diminishes as we move outward from the members of our family to our neighbors, our society, and the world. Traditionally, our sense of involvement with the fate of others has been in inverse proportion to the distance separating us and them.[2]

Scholar and social activist Chuck Collins defines his universe of obligation differently from the example Sacks offers. In the 1980s, Collins gave the half-million dollars that he inherited from his family to charity. Collins told journalist Ian Parker:

> Of course, we have to respond to our immediate family, but, once they're O.K., we need to expand the circle. A larger sense of family is a radical idea, but we get into trouble as a society when we don't see that we're in the same boat.[3]

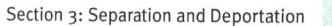

---

1 Helen Fein, *Accounting for Genocide* (New York: Free Press, 1979), 4.
2 Jonathan Sacks, *The Dignity of Difference: How to Avoid the Clash of Civilizations* (London: Continuum, 2002), 30.
3 Ian Parker, "The Gift," *New Yorker*, August 2, 2004, 60.

Connection Questions

1. What factors influence the way a society defines its universe of obligation? In what ways might a nation or community signal who is part of its universe of obligation and who is not?

2. What do you think might be some of the consequences for those who are not within a society's universe of obligation?

3. What factors influence how an individual defines his or her universe of obligation? In what ways might an individual show others who is part of his or her universe of obligation and who is not?

4. In the 1800s, sociologist William Graham Sumner wrote, "Every man and woman in society has one big duty. That is, to take care of his or her own self." Do you agree with Sumner? Why or why not? Is it wrong to prioritize caring for those closest to you over others? How does Sumner's suggestion about how we define our universe of obligation differ from Chuck Collins's view?

5. How would you describe your nation's universe of obligation? Your school's? Your own?

Universe of Obligation

In Circle 1, write your name.

In Circle 2, write the name of people to whom you feel the greatest obligation. For whom would you be willing to take a great risk or put yourself in peril? (You don't have to write actual names.)

In Circle 3, write the names of people who are on the next level—that is, people to whom you have some obligation, but not as great as for those in Circle 2.

In Circle 4, write the names of people who are on the next level—that is, people to whom you have some obligation, but not as great as for those in Circle 3.

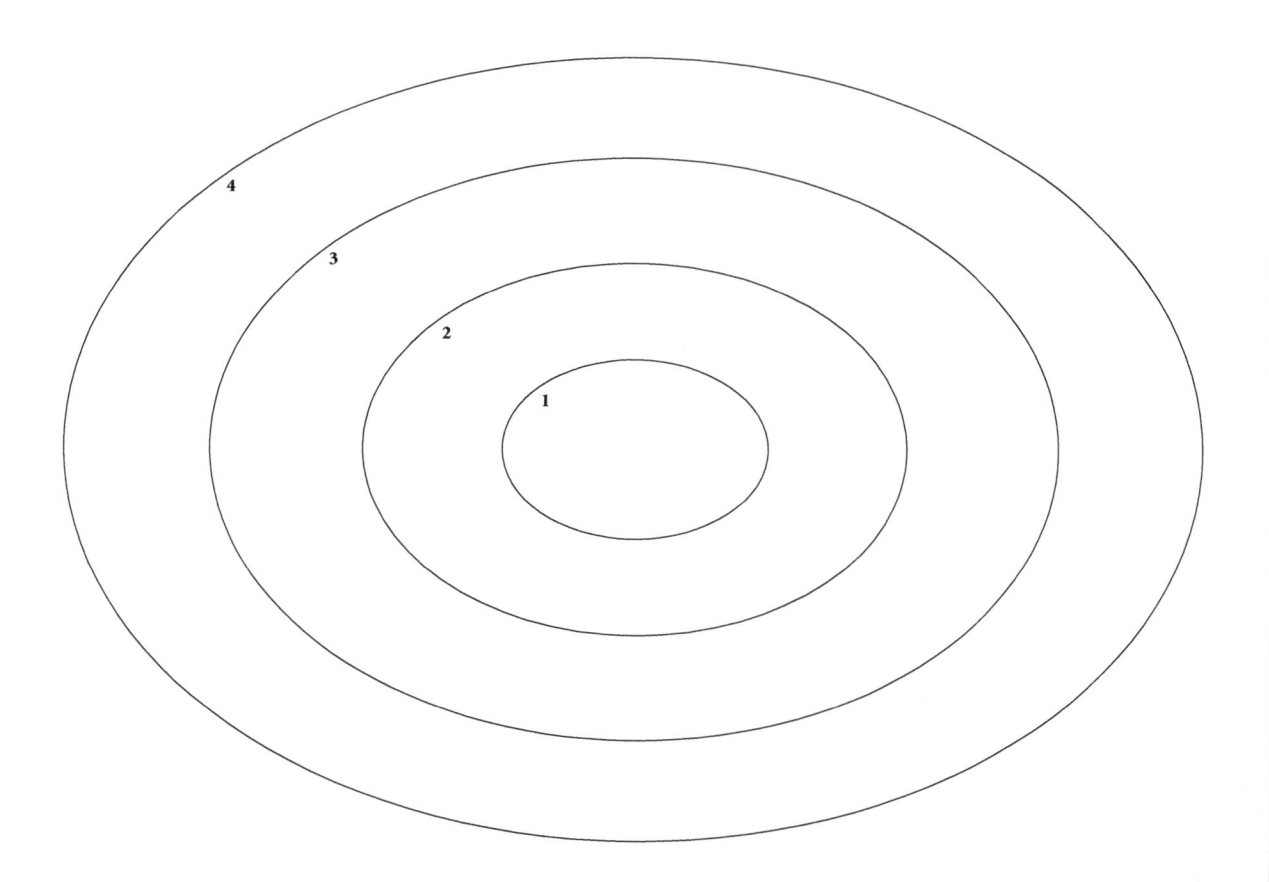

Witnesses, Bystanders, and Beneficiaries in Hungary

In *The Holocaust in Hungary: Evolution of a Genocide*, historians Zoltán Vági, László Csösz, and Gábor Kádár describe how non-Jews in Hungary reacted to the treatment of their Jewish neighbors under German occupation:

> According to the 1941 census, 15.48 million people lived in Hungary. More than 94 percent of them were non-Jewish. In 1944 the vast majority of this population passively observed the maltreatment of their Jewish compatriots. Only a small minority stood up against the persecution. The number of those civilians who actively participated in the Holocaust by reporting and abusing Jews was likewise small. In 1944–1945, thousands delivered food and messages to ghettos and collection camps and rescued their friends or complete strangers. Thousands of others reported the Jewish neighbors they envied, the boss they hated, or people they knew nothing about. Tens of thousands visited the board fence of the ghetto to peer inside or voiced content at seeing crowds headed towards the train station; at the same time tens of thousands most likely pitied the Jews' plight. But millions simply lived their lives, went to work, and tried to get by under the deteriorating conditions of war. They paid no attention to the tragedy unfolding around them.[1]

Many Hungarians hoped to benefit from the deportations by taking over Jewish property left behind, including businesses and apartments. In the capital of Budapest, where housing was in short supply, residents were so eager to claim the apartments of deported Jews that they overwhelmed the housing department charged with redistributing the apartments. In the summer of 1944, a local newspaper reported,

> The housing department of the capital [Budapest] has been overrun by such massive crowds of people that highly undesirable mob scenes have developed . . . City leaders have on several occasions asked the public not to rush to the housing bureau, for the assignment of apartments is suspended until further notice . . . The inventory of abandoned Jewish apartments is under way, and satisfactory steps will be taken within a short time to address those claiming apartments.[2]

Not all Hungarians sought to benefit from the deportations. Throughout 1944, journalist and author Sándor Márai kept a diary where he recorded the events he saw unfolding around him. Márai was a Christian intellectual who opposed the treatment of Hungary's Jews; he was also married to a woman of Jewish ancestry whose elderly father was deported to a camp in Poland. In May of 1944, the same month that Elie Wiesel and his family were deported to Auschwitz, Márai wrote,

> Nothing helps: everything must be experienced in person, on our own bodies. That is how we will understand it in reality. All that we have heard about the fate of Polish, Austrian, German Jews over the years was just a hazy image. But when I first saw a man being taken away to a truck by two Gestapo soldiers—on Vörösmarty

---

1   Zoltán Vági, László Csösz, and Gábor Kádár, *The Holocaust in Hungary: Evolution of a Genocide,* Documenting Life and Destruction: Holocaust Sources in Context series, United States Holocaust Memorial Museum Center for Advanced Holocaust Studies (Lanham: Alta Mira Press, 2013), 279.
2   Quoted in ibid., 287–88.

Square in Budapest—I understood reality. And now that men, women, children bearing yellow stars are marching along in front of my window, carrying their meager packages, to live crammed together, five thousand of them, tens of thousands of them, headed to some uncertain fate—I am afraid it is not really uncertain! . . . [N]ow I finally understand. All this has to be seen, in person . . .

It is shameful to be alive. It is shameful to be walking in the sun. It is shameful to be alive.[3]

---

[3] Quoted in ibid., 293.

Night and Day

Using the chart below, track Elie Wiesel's references to "night" and "day" throughout the memoir. Reflect on the meaning of each reference and on his use of the terms as a whole.

Which word?	Page number	Copy down a few lines that surround the word.	How might Wiesel be using this word as a symbol at this moment?
Example: Night	18	"Where were the people being taken? Did anyone know yet? No, the secret was well kept. Night had fallen."	They want answers but the night came, and it felt like doors and answers were closed to them.

Connection Questions

1. What do these words suggest in the early pages of the book?
2. How does their meaning change as the story unfolds?
3. What impact do they have on the reader?
4. How does Wiesel use this literary device to animate his story and amplify his message?

Found Poem: Mrs. Schächter's Vision

Create a found poem using only words, phrases, and quotations that have been selected and rearranged the scene in *Night* involving Mrs. Schächter's outburst in the cattle car. To create your poem, choose language that is particularly meaningful or interesting to you and organize that language around a theme or message.

1. Read the scene (from "There was a woman among us . . ." on page 24 to " . . . We had arrived in Birkenau" on page 28) two or three times. Read it out loud at least once.

2. While reading the scene one additional time, copy down 15 to 20 words and short phrases from it that you find memorable, powerful, or revealing.

3. Arrange the words and phrases you have selected into a poem. You might want to copy the words and phrases onto notecards or separate slips of paper so that you can easily rearrange them. Try to arrange the words in a way that captures what you think is the essence of the scene, as well as your experience of hearing it.

4. Here are a few more guidelines for creating your poem:

    - You DON'T have to use all of the words and phrases you chose.
    - You CAN repeat words or phrases.
    - You CAN'T add other words besides those you copied from the excerpt.
    - Your poem DOESN'T have to rhyme.

5. When you are satisfied with your poem, give it a title.

SECTION 4

AUSCHWITZ-BIRKENAU

Reading Assignment

Pages 29–46

Overview

This section of the memoir begins as the terrible train journey from Sighet is ending. Eliezer, his family, and the Jews of Sighet have arrived at Birkenau, a reception center for the vast concentration camp and killing center of Auschwitz. When the transport arrives at the station, the first thing people notice is fire. Flames are gushing out of huge chimneys against a black sky. An SS officer orders "Men to the left! Women to the right!" and Eliezer and his father are immediately separated from his mother and sisters. Eliezer describes horrific scenes of murder and death, but he and his father survive the selection process. As they are marched away, the "veteran" prisoners are amazed and angry to discover that the newcomers have never heard of Auschwitz.

Almost immediately, an initiation begins. Eliezer and his father are stripped of their belongings, their hair, even their names. They are pushed from place to place, beaten, and humiliated without explanation. Eventually they are taken from Birkenau to Auschwitz, where an officer tells them that they must work or go to the crematorium. A Polish prisoner quietly advises them to "help one another. It is the only way to survive." Three weeks later, they are moved yet again, this time to another part of the Auschwitz complex—a slave labor camp called Buna.

The events in this section of the memoir pose deep challenges for readers, who must struggle to imagine and confront a world that defies description. We encourage teachers to provide ample time for discussion and to use some of the strategies for processing emotionally powerful material described on page 3.

> Locate Auschwitz-Birkenau on the map "Eliezer's Forced Journey."

Exploring the Text

Ask students for their questions or comments about what they have read in this section. Then use the following questions as journal or discussion prompts to guide students' exploration of the text.

1. Why does Eliezer say that he left behind his "illusions," along with his belongings, when he got out of the train at Auschwitz? What "illusions" is he referring to?

2. Wiesel writes, "Eight words spoken quietly, indifferently, without emotion. Eight simple, short words. Yet that was the moment when I left my mother." What words is he speaking of? Why does he emphasize them? What does this moment reveal about the world of the camp?

3. How do the veteran inmates and others imprisoned in the camp treat the new arrivals? How do you account for their attitudes and actions?

4. How do the Germans orchestrate the arrival of new prisoners at Auschwitz? What are some of the key stages of this process? What is its purpose?

5. What questions do Eliezer and the other inmates ask of each other and themselves as they enter the camp? What lies or fictions do they tell themselves and others, and how does this influence their survival?

6. Why do you think the Germans take away the inmates' personal belongings? Their clothing? Why do they cut off their hair and tattoo a number on each person's arm? What effect does this process have on Eliezer? How do you think it affects the German guards?

7. How does Eliezer respond when his father is beaten for the first time? How does that response affect the way he sees himself? How might his universe of obligation be changing, and why?

8. In what ways has the environment at Auschwitz made Eliezer see himself and the world differently? What are some key words and phrases that reflect how his identity is changing? Add these quotations and ideas to your identity timeline for Eliezer.

> **Record an event on your identity timeline.**

9. Where in this section of the text do you see evidence of humanity in Auschwitz, despite the Nazi policies and practices of dehumanization?

10. Recounting the first night in the concentration camp, Wiesel writes, "Never shall I forget that night, the first night in the camp, that has turned my life into one long night . . ." (page 34). What does it mean for a life to be turned into "one long night"? What other references to "night" have you found in this section of the memoir? Add them to your Night and Day graphic organizer on page 42 and reflect on their meaning.

Connecting to the Central Question

After exploring the text and reviewing the events that take place in this section of the book, give students an opportunity to revisit their thinking about this guide's central question:

Q: *How is our identity shaped and reshaped by the circumstances we encounter? How do tragedy and trauma influence an individual's identity and choices?*

> **Refer to your identity timeline.**

Give students a few minutes to reflect and write in their journals about the changes they are noticing in Eliezer's identity during his initiation to Auschwitz. If you are having students use identity timelines, they may help in this reflection. Do the students' observations about Eliezer's changing identity support their previous thinking about the central question? Or do they prompt them to revise their thinking?

Activities for Deeper Understanding

1. Explore Arrival at Auschwitz through Images

This section of *Night* describes the arrival of Eliezer and the Jews of Sighet at Auschwitz. Wiesel tells a singular and deeply personal story, but this experience of arrival was shared by hundreds of thousands of Jews and other prisoners deported to Auschwitz. The Auschwitz Album visual essay includes selections from a famous collection of photographs of a transport arriving from Hungary in early summer 1944. The album was discovered by then-18-year-old Lilly Jacob in a vacant SS barracks on the day of her liberation in the Dora concentration camp, hundreds of miles from Auschwitz. Within its pages, she was shocked to find pictures of herself, her family, and her friends on the day of their arrival at Auschwitz.

Introduce the album to students and explain that you'll be making connections between the photographs and the events they've just read about in *Night* using the Crop It teaching strategy.

a. Before class, cut out pairs of *L*-shaped "cropping tools" to use for this activity. In class, give each student a pair of cropping tools and show them how to use them to focus on a particular detail of a photograph or other image; the tools can be adjusted to crop large sections of an image or to focus on a tiny detail.

b. Now provide copies of the Auschwitz Album visual essay. Explain the origin of the Auschwitz Album and give students time to look at all of the images. Then ask them to choose one photograph for this activity. Offer a series of prompts, one at a time, giving students a few moments on their own to crop a detail of the photograph in response. Silence and slow, deliberate pacing will help students to engage deeply with the image in front of them.

- Crop to show the part of the image that first caught your eye.
- Crop to show something you have a question about.
- Crop to show a detail that reveals when and where this image was taken.
- Crop to show a detail that connects to Eliezer's story in *Night*.
- Crop to show the most important part of the image.

c. After students work on their own, give them time to journal about some of the details they selected, and then invite them to discuss with a partner why they cropped those particular details.

d. As a class, discuss how the images connect to *Night*, using the Connect, Extend, Challenge teaching strategy. What details did students see in the images that also appear in the memoir? How did the memoir help them to interpret the images? How do the images deepen their understanding of the memoir? What do they feel, see, or understand that they did not before? Invite students to select one quotation from the memoir to use as a caption for their photograph.

2. Examine the "Moral Universe" of Auschwitz

The setting of this section of *Night* is the vast concentration camp and killing center of Auschwitz-Birkenau in the spring of 1944, when thousands of people were arriving daily and the SS gassed more than 6,000 Jews each day. To grasp this setting, readers need to do more than simply establish the time and place. They also need to probe the "moral universe" of the camp.

In any work of literature, the "moral universe" refers to the "rules, constraints, possibilities, potential conflicts and potential consequences"[1] that affect the choices the characters make. The "moral universe" includes power hierarchies and systems of values, norms, and expectations. Understanding the moral universe of a place like Auschwitz-Birkenau, or the settings of other works of Holocaust literature, presents a particular challenge because the shocking violence and cruelty of these places defies our norms of human behavior and eludes our attempts to explain or understand it. Even those who were there struggle to describe what it was like. As Elie Wiesel himself said, "Only those who were there will ever know, and those who were there can never tell."[2]

Despite these challenges, a focus on the moral universe of *Night* provides the essential context for understanding the pressures on Eliezer's identity, the conflicts he faces, and the limited choices he is able to make. To help students understand the distorted moral universe of Auschwitz, they can review a range of sources that reflect the experiences and points of view of victims, survivors, and perpetrators; each offers a distinct insight into the moral universe and the choices individuals made there. You can use some or all of these sources, depending on the time you have available, your goals, and the needs of your students.

Moral Universe

hierarchies
values taboos
beliefs expectations
norms obligations
constraints rules

a. Introduce the idea of a "moral universe" to your students. You might ask them to first journal about the moral universe of the community they live in. How would they describe the norms, values, hierarchies, and expectations that shape their everyday world?

b. Ask students to draw on their reading of *Night*, the Auschwitz Album visual essay, and the readings Auschwitz and A Commandant's View to describe the moral universe of Auschwitz. What specific details or quotations from the different images and texts illuminate the moral universe of the camp? Gather students' ideas into a

---

1 Michael W. Smith and Jeffrey D. Wilhelm, *Fresh Takes on Teaching Literary Elements* (New York: Scholastic, 2010), 25.
2 Quoted in Walter Laqueur and Judith Tydor Baumel, eds., *The Holocaust Encyclopedia* (New Haven: Yale University Press, 2001), 208.

web on a large sheet of paper that you can save and refer to as you continue to read the memoir. Then discuss the following:

- What events, ideas, or themes were consistent across all of the sources?
- What does each type of source contribute to your understanding? Which type of source is most impactful for you, and why?
- How does thinking about the moral universe of Auschwitz help you to reflect on the central question for our study of *Night*?

> Q: *How is our identity shaped and reshaped by the circumstances we encounter? How do tragedy and trauma influence an individual's identity and choices?*

3. Compare Holocaust Memoirs

Night is perhaps the most famous among thousands of Holocaust memoirs. Survivors' desire to tell their stories is often tempered, however, by a conviction that those who weren't "there"—in the ghetto, in hiding, in the camps—will never truly understand. Sonia Weitz, a poet who survived five camps, prefaced her own memoir by asking,

> But how does one bear witness to the unspeakable? . . . Normal standards do not apply to the Holocaust. Even language fails and words like *hunger, fear, hot, cold,* and *pain* lose their meaning. In fact, the Holocaust is a crime without a language.[3]

When we compare different Holocaust survivors' memoirs, we can more clearly see the varying ways these authors have used language to convey experiences that are, as Sonia Weitz says, "unspeakable." The reading Voices from Auschwitz: Charlotte Delbo provides an excerpt from the memoir of Charlotte Delbo, *None of Us Will Return*. We suggest pairing this text with a shorter excerpt from *Night* to compare and contrast how Delbo and Wiesel write about their experiences. One recommended excerpt from *Night* begins at the top of page 33 ("What a shame, a shame that you did not go with your mother") and goes to the middle of page 36 ("without any hope of finding either").

The following questions can help students read carefully and compare and contrast the two authors. Some questions could also be the basis for a student writing assignment.

- How does Delbo allude to the difficulty of describing her experiences? How is that similar to or different from Wiesel's approach?
- How does each text reveal the moral universe of Auschwitz?
- What is the point of view of each author?
- To whom is each text addressed?
- How do Delbo and Wiesel use imagery, allusion, diction, and syntax to convey their experiences?
- What distinct insights come from each text? Which text is most meaningful to you?

---

3 Sonia Schreiber Weitz, *I Promised I Would Tell* (Brookline, MA: Facing History and Ourselves, Inc., 2012), x.

The Auschwitz Album

"The Ramp"

Women and children arrive on the "ramp" at Birkenau, where they would be moved along toward the gates. There, physicians decided whether they were fit for slave labor or death.

Arrival at Birkenau

Mass scene of Jews arriving after an arduous journey. Here they would face the selection process, which ended for many in the crematorium that can be seen in the background.

Selection Process

The start of the selection process, in front of the camp's entrance. Some prisoners who had already been at the camp for a time were made to assist in sorting the new arrivals.

Crematoria IV and V

A group of women and children going toward Crematoria IV and V. There they would be killed, as they were considered to be too weak to do hard labor.

Confiscation of Prisoners' Belongings

A trailer full of the clothes and luggage of new prisoners passes a group of women, who are presumably heading toward the gas chamber.

Selected for Slave Labor

These men were determined fit to perform hard labor. Their heads were shaved and their clothes replaced with prison uniforms.

Auschwitz

In 1940, the Nazis built a camp called Auschwitz, located about 37 miles west of Kraków, Poland, to imprison Soviet prisoners of war and Polish resisters. In October 1941, the Nazis built a second camp there, known as Auschwitz II, or Auschwitz-Birkenau. With four large crematoria (including gas chambers and ovens to cremate victims' bodies), Auschwitz-Birkenau became the largest of the killing centers built by the Nazis. Jews from all over Europe were sent to Auschwitz to be murdered. Some have said that the system of killing there resembled an industrial production line—but at Auschwitz, the goal of the process was not the production of goods but the deaths of millions of people.

The process began when Jews were ordered out of the trains that brought them to the death camp and made to stand in line for the "selection," in which a Nazi doctor or other official would quickly decide which prisoners could serve as slave laborers and which would be killed right away. Small children and women with children were not considered for labor but automatically selected to be killed. Those not selected for labor were told that they would first undress and go into a special room for a shower and disinfection, after which they would be given food and new clothing. In reality, the shower rooms were gas chambers.

Some Jews were deliberately kept alive to assist with the killing process. Formed into *Sonderkommandos*, or special detachments, they were the ones who told the new arrivals to undress and then led them to the "shower room." The Sonderkommandos were under strict orders to say nothing to the victims about what really awaited them. After the poison gas was released into the chambers and everyone inside was dead, the Sonderkommandos removed the bodies and transported them to specially built crematoria to be burned. Every few months, the Sonderkommandos were themselves murdered and replaced by a new group of prisoners.

A former Sonderkommando member described the killing process this way, beginning with the undressing hall:

> The people walked into the room and once they were all inside they began to undress.... From the undressing room the people went down a narrow corridor to the gas chamber. At the entrance, there was a sign: "To the Disinfection Room." ...[T]he men waited naked until the women were in the gas chamber, and then they went in.... When a large transport with lots of people came, the people were beaten to force them to enter the room.... Only when they were already in the gas chamber did they sense that something was out of whack. When the gas chamber filled up, the Germans stood at the door with dogs and continued to pack the people in so that more than were already inside could be gassed. Those who hadn't gone in yet began to shout. The Germans responded with murderous beatings. The people were already naked and defenseless, so they were pushed in by force....
> The moment the gas chamber filled up the SS man closed the door. Right after that, SS men drove over in a car that carried the emblem of the Red Cross. The cans of gas were taken out of the car, opened, and their contents were thrown into the gas chambers through the opening of the wall.... Some time later, the SS doctor

determined the death of the people in the chamber by saying "It's all over." Then he drove away in the "Red Cross" car.[1]

As historians and survivors have struggled to describe and understand the nature of death camps like Auschwitz, they have also emphasized the near impossibility of conveying what it was like to people who were not there. Historian Gideon Greif, who edited a book of Sonderkommando accounts, writes:

> Many former prisoners explained in their testimonies that everyday life in the Nazi camps was based on a total reversal of all moral standards. Power was associated solely with the license to oppress and torture. Values such as mercy and compassion were regarded as extreme, negative and perverse. . . . It gave rise to an upside-down world or, as the writer and Auschwitz survivor K. Tzetnik put it, "another planet," a place that functioned on different, unknown principles. . . . Auschwitz constituted a reality that had never before existed and had never been known, let alone experienced.[2]

---

[1] Gideon Greif, *We Wept Without Tears: Testimonies of the Jewish Sonderkommando from Auschwitz* (New Haven: Yale University Press, 2005), 153–55.
[2] Ibid., 52–53.

A Commandant's View

In 1971, journalist Gitta Sereny interviewed Franz Stangl, who had been the commandant of the death camp at Sobibór and, later, the camp at Treblinka.

"Would it be true to say that you were used to the liquidations?"
He thought for a moment. "To tell the truth," he then said, slowly and thoughtfully, "one did become used to it."

"In days? Weeks? Months?"
"Months. It was months before I could look one of them in the eye. I repressed it all by trying to create a special place: gardens, new barracks, new kitchens, new everything: barbers, tailors, shoemakers, carpenters. There were hundreds of ways to take one's mind off it; I used them all."

"Even so, if you felt that strongly, there had to be times, perhaps at night, in the dark, when you couldn't avoid thinking about it."
"In the end, the only way to deal with it was to drink. I took a large glass of brandy to bed with me each night and I drank."

"I think you are evading my question."
"No, I don't mean to; of course, thoughts came. But I forced them away. I made myself concentrate on work, work, and again work."

"Would it be true to say that you finally felt they weren't really human beings?"
"When I was on a trip once, years later in Brazil," he said, his face deeply concentrated and obviously reliving the experience, "my train stopped next to a slaughterhouse. The cattle in the pens, hearing the noise of the train, trotted up to the fence and stared at the train. They were very close to my window, one crowding the other, looking at me through that fence. I thought then, 'Look at this; this reminds me of Poland; that's just how the people looked, trustingly, just before they went into the tins...'"

"You said tins," I interrupted. *"What do you mean?"* But he went on without hearing, or answering me.
"... I couldn't eat tinned meat after that. Those big eyes... which looked at me ... not knowing that in no time at all they'd all be dead." He paused. His face was drawn. At this moment he looked old and worn and sad.

"So you didn't feel they were human beings?"
"Cargo," he said tonelessly. "They were cargo." He raised and dropped his hand in a gesture of despair. Both our voices had dropped. It was one of the few times in those weeks of talks that he made no effort to cloak his despair, and his hopeless grief allowed a moment of sympathy.

"When do you think you began to think of them as cargo? The way you spoke earlier, of the day when you first came to Treblinka, the horror you felt seeing the dead bodies everywhere—they weren't 'cargo' to you then, were they?"
"I think it started the day I first saw the Totenlager [death camp] in Treblinka. I remember [Christian Wirth, the man who set up the death camps] standing there

next to the pits full of blue-black corpses. It had nothing to do with humanity—it couldn't have; it was a mass—a mass of rotting flesh. Wirth said, 'What shall we do with this garbage?' I think unconsciously that started me thinking of them as cargo."

"There were so many children; did they ever make you think of your children, of how you would feel in the position of those parents?"
"No," he said slowly, "I can't say I ever thought that way." He paused. "You see," he then continued, still speaking with this extreme seriousness and obviously intent on finding a new truth within himself, "I rarely saw them as individuals. It was always a huge mass. I sometimes stood on the wall and saw them in the tube. But—how can I explain it—they were naked, packed together, running, being driven with whips like . . . " The sentence trailed off.

. . . *"Could you not have changed that?" I asked. "In your position, could you not have stopped the nakedness, the whips, the horror of the cattle pens?"*
"No, no, no. This was the system. . . . It worked. And because it worked, it was irreversible."[1]

---

1   Gitta Sereny, *Into that Darkness: An Examination of Conscience* (London: Pan Books, 1977), 200–02.

Voices from Auschwitz: Charlotte Delbo

Charlotte Delbo (1913–1985) was a member of the French resistance, along with her husband, Georges Dudach. Neither was Jewish. Both were arrested in March 1942 by French police who were collaborating with the Nazis. While Dudach was executed on French soil, Delbo was deported in January 1943 to Auschwitz. This excerpt comes from Delbo's collection of post-war writings, *None of Us Will Return*.

Street for Arrivals, Street for Departures

There are people arriving. They scan the crowd of those who wait seeking those who wait for them. They kiss them and they say that they are tired from the journey.

There are people leaving. They say good-by to those who are not leaving and they kiss the children.

There is a street for people arriving and a street for people leaving.

There is a café called "Arrivals" and a café called "Departures."

There are people arriving and there are people leaving.

But there is a station where those arriving are the same as those leaving
a station at which those arriving have never arrived, to which those leaving have never returned
it is the biggest station in the world.

This is the station at which they arrive, wherever they come from.

They arrive here after days and nights
after crossing whole countries
they arrive here with children, even babies, who were not supposed to have been taken

They have brought their children because you do not part with children for this journey.

Those who had gold brought it along because they thought gold might be useful.

Everyone brought his dearest possession because you must not leave what is dear to you when you go far away.

Everyone has brought his life along, above all it was his life that he had to bring along.

And when they arrive
they think they have arrived
in Hell
possibly. Still they do not believe it.

They did not know that you could take a train to Hell but since they are here, they steel themselves and feel ready to face it
with women, children, aged parents
with family keepsakes and family documents.

They do not know that you do not arrive at that station.

They expect the worst—they do not expect the unthinkable.

And when the soldiers shout to them to line up by fives, men on one side, women and children on the other, in a language they do not understand, they understand the blows of the truncheon and line up by fives since they are ready for anything.

Mothers clutch their children—they shudder at the thought that the children might be taken away from them—because the children are hungry and thirsty and crumpled from not having slept across so many lands. At long last they are arriving, they will be able to take care of them.

And when the soldiers shout to them to leave bundles and blankets and keepsakes on the platform they leave them because they ought to be ready for anything and do not wish to be surprised at anything. They say "We'll see"; they have already seen so much and they are tired from the journey.

The station is not a station. It is the end of a line. They look and they are stricken by the desolation about them.

In the morning, fog hides the marshes.

In the evening, spotlights illuminate the white barbed-wire fences with the sharpness of stellar photography. They believe that this is where they are being taken, and they are terrified.

At night, they wait for daylight with the children weighing down their mothers' arms. Wait and wonder.

In the daytime they do not wait. The lines start moving right away. Women and children first, they are the most weary. The men next. They are also weary but relieved that their wives and children are being taken care of first.

For the women and children always go first.

In the winter they are gripped by the cold. Especially those who come from Crete. Snow is new to them.

In the summer the sun blinds them as they step down from the dark boxcars that were sealed shut at the start of the journey.

At the start of the journey from France from the Ukraine from Albania from Belgium from Slovakia from Italy from Hungary from the Peloponnesus from Holland from Macedonia from Austria from Herzegovina from the shores of the Black Sea from the shores of the Baltic from the shores of the Mediterranean and from the banks of the Vistula.

They would like to know where they are. They do not know that this is the center of Europe. They look for the name of the station. It is a station without a name.

A station which for them will never have a name.[1]

---

[1] Charlotte Delbo, *None of Us Will Return*, trans. John Githens (Boston: Beacon Press, 1968), 5–13, 128.

SECTION 5

MORAL COMPLEXITY

Reading Assignment

Pages 47–65

Overview

As this section begins, Eliezer and his father are selected for slave labor and moved once again, this time to Buna/Monowitz, a satellite camp of Auschwitz owned by the German industrial firm IG Farben. Eliezer and his father endure routine humiliations and random violence at the hands of both German officers and *kapos*, prisoners assigned to assist in the running of the camp. Eliezer's father finds it harder and harder to keep up, and Eliezer feels a troubling mixture of anger, love, and pity. As all the prisoners struggle with hunger, Eliezer says he is becoming nothing more than a "starved stomach." Although a public hanging briefly troubles him, he and the other men are too hungry to think much beyond their dinner. Then a child and two adult prisoners are hanged for hiding weapons. The other prisoners, forced to watch, feel a renewed despair. It is in this environment of moral, physical, and spiritual extremes that Eliezer, his father, and the other prisoners try to stay alive.

> **Locate Buna on the map "Eliezer's Forced Journey."**

The painful events of this section of the memoir can elicit powerful emotional responses and deep questions from students. We encourage teachers to take ample time for discussion and to use some of the strategies for processing emotionally powerful material described on page 3.

Exploring the Text

Ask students for their questions or comments about what they have read in this section. Then use the following questions as journal or discussion prompts to guide students' exploration of the text.

1. Give examples of the ways Eliezer's relationship with his father is changing. What is prompting those changes?

2. What does Eliezer mean when he refers to his father as his "weak point"? Why has he come to view love as a weakness?

3. What new relationships does Eliezer form in this section of the text? What do these relationships mean for him?

4. Who has authority at Buna? Where does that authority come from? How do those with authority use their power over others?

5. What happens to Eliezer's gold crown? Why does he try to keep it, and how does he ultimately lose it?

6. Trace the references to soup in this section of the text. How does Wiesel use references to soup to reveal something about the physical, moral, and spiritual conditions of life in the camp?

7. Eliezer describes two hangings in this section. He tells the reader that he witnessed many others, yet he chose to write only about these two. Why are these two hangings so significant for him? How do they differ from the others?

8. When the young boy is hanged, a prisoner asks, "For God's sake, where is God?" Eliezer hears a voice answer, "Where He is? This is where—hanging here from this gallows . . ." (page 65). What does this statement mean? Is it a statement of despair? Anger? Hope? (Note: The theme of faith and doubt is explored more fully in the next section of this guide.)

9. What words, phrases, and images from this section of the text reveal how Eliezer's identity is changing in response to what he is experiencing? Add these to your identity timeline.

Record an event on your identity timeline.

Connecting to the Central Question

After exploring the text and reviewing the events that take place in this section of the book, give students an opportunity to revisit their thinking about this guide's central question:

Q: *How is our identity shaped and reshaped by the circumstances we encounter? How do tragedy and trauma influence an individual's identity and choices?*

Give students a few minutes to reflect and write in their journals about the changes they are noticing in Eliezer's identity as a result of his harrowing experiences in Auschwitz. If you are having students use identity timelines, they may help in this reflection. Do the students' observations about Eliezer's changing identity support their previous thinking about the central question? Or do they prompt them to revise their thinking?

Refer to your identity timeline.

Activities for Deeper Understanding

1. Introduce Choiceless Choices

A story like *Night*, full of cruelty, violence, and dehumanization, demands ethical reflection. Yet the moral universe of Auschwitz (introduced in the last section) defies our standard norms of ethics and human behavior. Where we might expect sons to be loyal to fathers, we instead see Eliezer increasingly forced to choose between fidelity to his father and his own safety. Where we might expect members of victim groups to show solidarity with each other, we instead see some inmates' vicious behavior toward others. In Auschwitz, prisoners are forced into impossible choices and morally ambiguous roles that resist easy categorization as "right" and "wrong." We focus on these themes to reflect on the pressures on identity and human behavior in extremity, not to judge the morality of victims or to consider "what I would have done" in such circumstances.

Scholar Lawrence Langer introduced the term "choiceless choices" to describe prisoners' lack of true agency within the camps. This notion can illuminate many of the experiences described in this section of the memoir.

Have students explore this notion by responding to the reading Choiceless Choices using the Big Paper teaching strategy. Depending on the age and reading level of your students, you may first want to paraphrase Langer's definition and come to a shared understanding as a class before beginning the Big Paper activity. You can use the connection questions that follow the reading as prompts for students' silent conversation and follow-up class discussion.

2. Further Explore Moral Complexity

Moral complexity is also evident in Wiesel's descriptions of the *kapos* in the camp. Kapos were prisoners who were given a degree of privilege and authority over other prisoners to make the camp run smoothly. As we see through the figures of Idek and Franek in this section of *Night*, they could be both kind and extraordinarily vicious. The reading The Role of the Kapo includes insights from historians and commentary from Holocaust survivors, including Elie Wiesel and Primo Levi, about the difficulty of judging the actions of people like the kapos who acted in the roles of both victims and perpetrators.

Discuss The Role of the Kapo with students. You can either distribute the reading and hold a whole-group discussion using the questions below or use the Pick a Number teaching strategy to structure a more varied discussion. Students can use some of the following questions to guide their "pick a number" conversations about specific quotations from the reading.

- How does this source connect to *Night*? In what ways does it help you to understand the memoir?

- How did the Nazi policy of using some prisoners to control others influence the relationships between those who were held in the camps?

- How much agency did kapos have? How might you begin to account for the choices made by kapos in this section of *Night*?

- Wiesel writes, "Am I sure I would have kept my hands clean? No, I am not, and no one can be." Why do you think he says this? What is he suggesting about identity and human behavior?

- How do Wiesel and Levi want us to view the choices of kapos? Do you think it is possible to judge their behavior? Why or why not?

3. Examine Varieties of Resistance

The story Wiesel tells in this section of *Night* often reveals the desperation and powerlessness he and so many others experienced in the camps. Yet he also lets the reader see moments when the prisoners exercise agency to maintain a sense of dignity and humanity, and even to fight back against those who oppress them.

The reading Varieties of Resistance introduces the topic of resistance during the Holocaust, with a focus on the revolt at Auschwitz. In a companion video testimony

Resistances in Auschwitz (see hstry.is/TeachingNight), Anna Heilman describes her experience with this same revolt.

After students read the text and/or watch the video, ask them to reflect on these questions, either in class discussion, in pairs using the Think, Pair, Share teaching strategy, or as journal prompts:

- What does the word *resistance* mean to you? Some insist that armed resistance is the only form of legitimate resistance. Others stress the idea that resistance requires organization. Still others argue that resistance is more about the will to live and the power of hope than it is about either weapons or organization. Which view is closest to your own?

- Use your ideas about and definitions of resistance to decide which of the following is an act of resistance:

    - Eliezer's refusal to let the dentist remove his gold crown
    - Eliezer's decision to give up the crown to protect his father
    - The French girl's decision to speak in German to Eliezer after he is beaten
    - The prisoner's choice to die for soup
    - The prisoners' attempt to stockpile weapons, for which they are later hanged

- In each act of resistance that you identified, who or what are the prisoners resisting? Some scholars believe that the right question to ask about resistance is not why there were not more such acts but why there were any at all. What do you think is meant by that statement? Do you agree?

Choiceless Choices

Scholar Lawrence Langer introduced the term "choiceless choices" to describe prisoners' lack of true agency within the camps. He argues that behavior in the camps

> . . . cannot be viewed through the same lens we used to view normal human behavior since the rules of law and morality and the choices available for human decisions were not permitted in these camps for extermination. As important as it is to point out situations of dignity and morality which reinforce our notions of normal behavior, it is all the more important here to try to convey the "unimaginable," where surviving in extremity meant an existence that had no relation to our system of time and space and where physical survival under these conditions resulted in "choiceless choices"![1]

Connection Questions

1. How would you paraphrase Langer's idea of "choiceless choices"?
2. What examples of choiceless choices have you found in *Night*?
3. Have you seen any examples of the "dignity and morality" Langer references?
4. How does this concept add to your understanding of the experiences of victims and survivors of the Holocaust?
5. What is the relationship between our choices and our identity? What happens to identities in the absence of meaningful choices?
6. What new question does exploring this theme raise for you?

---

[1] Lawrence L. Langer, "The Dilemma of Choice in the Deathcamps," *Centerpoint: A Journal of Interdisciplinary Studies* 4, no. 1 (Fall 1980): 53–58.

The Role of the Kapo

1. In an article titled "Victims Who Victimise," law professor Mark Drumbl explains the role of the kapo within the Nazi camp system:

    Kapos were inmate functionaries whose day-to-day supervision enabled the camps, even sprawling ones, to run with comparatively few SS overseers. They were key cogs in the Nazi policy of 'prisoner self-administration'. *Kapos* exercised their limited agency at times in empathetic ways, at other times to resist, but also to hurt and savage others under their charge. *Kapos* themselves were hierarchically organized—from a chief *Kapo* down to the barrack commander (*Blockältester*) and even lower, ending with the *Sonderkommando*, those inmates engaged to extract teeth and shear hair—mutilations undertaken for the purposes of supplying the Reich—from the dead after the SS gassings and then to burn the bodies in the crematoria. . . . A detainee's status as a *Kapo* was fragile. Demotion was always possible. An erstwhile *Kapo* could be expelled back into the ranks of the ordinary prisoners, in which case he or she might face a most uncertain fate. Despite the contingency of their status, *Kapos* wielded enormous power over their subjects. Authority, after all, is situational.[1]

2. Historian Doris Bergen observes:

    The use of kapos encouraged the development of hierarchies of power within the camps. Such divisions, of course, benefited the Nazis, who needed to invest less time and energy to control prisoners who were at odds with one another. By rewarding kapos for brutality against fellow prisoners, German officials continued to undermine solidarity. Every kapo realized he or she could be replaced at a moment's notice. There were plenty of prisoners eager to improve their chances by accepting positions of privilege within the camp.[2]

3. In a later memoir, Elie Wiesel wrote about inmates who tried "to show the killers they could be just like them." He said,

    No one has the right to judge them, especially not those who did not experience Auschwitz or Buchenwald. The sages of our Tradition state point-blank: "Do not judge your fellow-man until you stand in his place." In other words, in the same situation, would I have acted as he did? Sometimes doubt grips me. Suppose I had spent not eleven months but eleven years in a concentration camp. Am I sure I would have kept my hands clean? No, I am not, and no one can be.[3]

4. Author Primo Levi, who also survived Auschwitz, also resisted the idea applying standard notions of moral judgment to the camps. He wrote,

    We now invite the reader to contemplate the possible meaning in the Lager [camp] of the words "good" and "evil," "just" and "unjust"; let everybody judge, on the basis of the picture we have outlined . . . how much of our ordinary moral world could survive on this side of the barbed wire.[4]

---

[1] Marc A. Drumbl, "Victims Who Victimise," *London Review of International Law* 4: 2 (2016): 217–46, https://academic.oup.com/lril/article/4/2/217/2222520/Victims-who-victimise.
[2] Doris Bergen, *War and Genocide: A Concise History of the Holocaust,* Third Edition (Lanham: Rowman and Littlefield Publishing Group, 2016), 219.
[3] Elie Wiesel, *All Rivers Run to the Sea: Memoirs* (New York: Knopf, 1995), 86–87.
[4] Primo Levi, *Survival in Auschwitz* (New York: Touchstone, 1996), 86.

Varieties of Resistance

Jewish resistance to Nazi oppression occurred throughout the Holocaust. In homes and schools, Jewish communities continued to observe religious rituals and holidays, educate their children in secular and religious schools, write, play music, and express their intellectual and artistic voices while defying the Nazi laws prohibiting such practices. The struggle to maintain a sense of identity, dignity, faith, and culture was a form of defiance, known today as "spiritual resistance."

At other times, resistance occurred through physical and armed struggle. Even in the most extreme of environments, such as the ghettos and the concentration and death camps, Jewish prisoners organized armed uprisings, risking their lives and those of their fellow prisoners. Professor Lawrence Langer explains:

> A group working outside the barbed-wire fences of the Sobibor death camp overpowered and killed the Ukrainian guards and escaped into the surrounding woods. The SS summoned all the remaining prisoners in the camp to roll call, and randomly chose every tenth one to be sent to the gas chamber. With what language or spirit do we admire the heroic daring of the escapees, once we have learned the effect of their flight? Does the life of the few "redeem" the death of the others? Or in celebrating one, do we defame the other? Neither query nor language begins to grasp the complexity of situations like these, which elude common definition and cast us into a morass of moral confusion.[1]

In Auschwitz, an armed uprising was organized and carried out by the 12th *Sonderkommando* unit working in Crematorium IV.[2] Jewish women such as Ester Wajcblum, Ella Gärtner, and Regina Safirsztain, who worked in the nearby Auschwitz munitions factory of Weichsel-Union Metallwerke, were the first in the chain of smugglers necessary for this uprising to occur. These women hid small amounts of gunpowder in bits of cloth, concealed them on and in their bodies, and passed them on to Rosa Robota, who worked in the clothing detail at Birkenau. She would then pass them on to her co-conspirators in the Sonderkommando, who would manufacture the crude explosives and primitive grenades used later to launch the attack.

On October 7, 1944, after learning that his Sonderkommando unit was to be murdered, Chaim Neuhof launched the revolt. Attacking SS guards in the crematoria with hammers and axes smuggled in, Neuhof and other members of the Sonderkommando fought back heroically, cutting fences, opening fire on the guards, and detonating explosives that were attached to captured SS guards, despite being woefully outnumbered. With superior arms and manpower, the Germans quickly suppressed the uprising. After being betrayed by one of the Sonderkommando, all five of the women were captured. Despite being tortured for months, they refused to reveal any remaining individuals involved in the uprising.

On January 5, 1945, all five were publicly hanged in front of the entire female camp population. It was the last public execution held at the camp. Twelve days later, German authorities forced all remaining prisoners, including Elie Wiesel and his father, to leave Auschwitz-Birkenau in order to flee from the advancing Soviet Red Army.

---

1 Lawrence Langer, *Art from the Ashes: A Holocaust Anthology* (Oxford: Oxford University Press, 1995), 6.
2 "Prisoner Revolt at Auschwitz-Birkenau," United States Holocaust Memorial Museum website, www.ushmm.org/learn/timeline-of-events/1942-1945/auschwitz-revolt.

SECTION 6

FAITH AND SURVIVAL

Reading Assignment

Pages 66–84

Overview

The previous section of *Night* ended with an inmate's anguished cry at the hanging of a young boy: "For God's sake, where is God?" (page 65). Questioning God amid the struggle to survive is a central theme of this section of the memoir, as Eliezer and other prisoners ask whether they can—or should—maintain their faith and rituals despite their suffering. On the eve of Rosh Hashanah, the Jewish New Year, prisoners improvise religious services and Eliezer attends, even though he feels like an outsider because he has begun to question God. For a person who once said he believed "profoundly," Eliezer's questioning of God is a signal of the drastic transformation of his identity. A few days later, he, his father, and the others in the camp debate whether to fast on Yom Kippur, the holiest day in the Jewish year—the Day of Atonement.

Not long after Yom Kippur, another "selection" is announced, and this time Eliezer's father is chosen. Preparing for the end, he gives his son his inheritance—a knife and a spoon. Eliezer spends the entire day fearing that his father has been taken away. However, when he returns that night, his father is still there. He has somehow made it through the final "selection." Those who did not are seemingly forgotten in the terrible days that follow—days when the prisoners receive "more blows than food." By January, Eliezer is in the camp infirmary with an infected foot, and he learns that the Soviet Red Army is approaching Buna and that the camp will be evacuated. For the first time in months, Eliezer and his father have a choice to make: they can leave with others or stay behind. They decide to leave. They are marched with the other prisoners through the icy countryside in the dead of winter to yet another unknown camp.

Exploring the Text

Ask students for their questions or comments about what they have read in this section. Then use the following questions as journal or discussion prompts to guide students' exploration of the text.

1. This section opens with the most significant holidays in the Jewish calendar, Rosh Hashanah (the Jewish New Year) and Yom Kippur (the Day of Atonement). What do these holidays mean for the prisoners at Buna? In what ways is their meaning similar to or different from their meaning before the war?

2. List some of the questions that Eliezer and other prisoners ask of God or about God in this section of the text. What do these questions reveal about different

characters' religious beliefs and how their experiences have influenced their faith?

3. On Rosh Hashanah, Eliezer says, "My eyes had opened and I was alone, terribly alone in a world without God, without man. Without love or mercy. I was nothing but ashes now . . ." (page 68). Eliezer is describing himself at a religious service attended by ten thousand men, including his own father. What do you think he means when he says that he is alone?

4. What other words, phrases, images, and metaphors signal how Eliezer's identity is changing, especially his religious identity? If you are keeping an identity timeline for Eliezer, add these quotations and ideas.

> **Record an event on your identity timeline.**

5. Why does Eliezer refuse to fast on Yom Kippur?

6. Why does Eliezer direct his anger toward God rather than the Germans? What does his anger suggest about the depths of his faith?

7. At the infirmary, another patient tells Eliezer, "I have more faith in Hitler than in anyone else. He alone has kept his promises, all his promises, to the Jewish people" (page 81). What is the patient saying about Hitler? What is he suggesting about his faith in God?

8. Why does Eliezer describe himself as "afraid" of having to wish his father a happy New Year? Describe the encounter between father and son after the services. Why does Eliezer say that the two of them "had never understood one another so clearly"?

9. Why did his father give him the spoon and the knife as his inheritance? What is the significance of such a gift in Auschwitz?

10. Consider how Eliezer and his father make a decision that will decide their fate. What choices are open to Eliezer and his father when the camp is evacuated? How do they decide? How might their experience help you understand why so many Holocaust survivors attribute their survival to luck or chance?

Connecting to the Central Question

After exploring the text and reviewing the events that take place in this section of the book, give students an opportunity to revisit their thinking about this guide's central question:

Q: *How is our identity shaped and reshaped by the circumstances we encounter? How do tragedy and trauma influence an individual's identity and choices?*

> **Refer to your identity timeline.**

Give students a few minutes to reflect and write in their journals about the changes they are noticing in Eliezer's identity, including his religious identity, as a result of his experiences in Auschwitz. If you are having students use identity timelines, they may help in this reflection. Do the students' observations about Eliezer's changing identity support their previous thinking about the central question? Or do they prompt them to revise their thinking?

Activities for Deeper Understanding

1. Explore Themes of Faith and Doubt

Many of the central figures in *Night*, including Wiesel himself, are people for whom faith, religious study, and ritual observance are at the heart of their lives. Among the many conflicts and tragedies in Wiesel's story is the way that the Holocaust unsettles or even destroys their religious identities and beliefs. For believers, the Holocaust raised painful questions, some of which Wiesel voices in his memoir: How could a good and all-powerful God allow this to happen?

Such questions are shared by many survivors, and indeed by many people who study the events of the Holocaust. But not all survivors answered these questions in the same way as Wiesel, who writes in *Night* of the flames that "consumed my faith forever" and the moments that "murdered my God and my soul" (page 34). Wiesel himself revisited questions of faith and doubt in many other works that he wrote after *Night*. Distribute the reading Faith after the Holocaust, an excerpt from David Weiss Halivni's memoir *The Book and the Sword*, as a complement to *Night*. Use the Connect, Extend, Challenge teaching strategy to help students compare and contrast the two authors:

- How does each author experience religious life and rituals in the camps?

- How would you describe each author's faith and relationship to God?

- What do these readings tell you about how the two authors' experiences of the Holocaust shaped their religious faith?

2. Explore Faith and Doubt through Art

Similar questions are raised in artist Samuel Bak's painting *Creation of War Time*. Bak's artistic talents were celebrated when he was still a child; when he was nine, his drawings were exhibited in the ghetto in Vilna (a city near the disputed 1930s border between Poland and Lithuania). He survived the Holocaust and went on to create a vast body of work that explores themes of identity and loss, memory and history. Creation of War Time can deepen students' thinking about the themes of faith and doubt in *Night*, particularly when compared to Michelangelo's painting Creation of Adam.

Professor Lawrence Langer's interpretation of the two works, in the reading Quotations about Michelangelo's and Bak's Work, can help you prepare to lead a discussion on the painting with your students. If your students are more advanced readers, you might share this reading with them directly.

Begin this activity by projecting the image of Bak's Creation of War Time on a large screen or by distributing color copies to each student or pair of students. Then take the class through the following analysis process step by step.

- Ask students exactly what they see in the painting. List their observations on the board. If students begin to offer interpretations, remind them to hold their ideas for later in the exercise. At this point, they are to focus on what they actually see.

- Use the students' list of observations to begin their interpretation of the painting.

    - For example, what colors does Bak use to paint a particular object or person?

- Why might he have chosen those colors?
- How do those colors affect the mood of the painting?
- Where is the object or person located in the picture?
- Why might Bak have painted that person or object there?
- Why do you think Bak chose to place certain objects or people in the foreground while others are in the background?

- What does the title of the painting, *Creation of War Time*, mean? What is the message of the painting? Ask students to write a brief interpretation in their journals.

Next, compare Bak's painting to Michelangelo's Creation of Adam from the Sistine Chapel by distributing or projecting the image. Explain to students that *Creation of War Time* was inspired at least in part by Michelangelo's work. Remind them that Michelangelo was an artist who lived in what is now Italy about 500 years ago (1475–1564). His work often featured biblical characters and stories.

Have students examine the Michelangelo work in much the way they studied Bak's painting. Then ask students to consider the following questions:

- How are the two paintings alike? How do they differ? (Encourage students to look for similarities and differences in the images that the two paintings feature, the mood each conveys, and the positioning of the two main figures.)
- In Michelangelo's painting, there is a very specific figure on the right. Who is that figure? How does Bak show that figure in his painting? Why do you think he chose to draw that image in that particular way? How does that decision affect the message the painting sends?

Ask students to relate the paintings to their reading of *Night*:

- What questions do you think Samuel Bak is asking about God through his painting? Are these questions similar to or different from the questions Wiesel asks in *Night*?
- Choose a quotation from this section of *Night* to pair with Bak's painting. Why did you choose this quotation? How does it connect to something specific in Bak's work?
- How do you think Elie Wiesel would interpret Bak's painting? If you read the excerpt from David Weiss Halivni's memoir, how do you think he would interpret the painting? Would Wiesel's and Halivni's interpretations be similar or different?

3. Make Space for Reflection

The painful events of this section of the memoir and the companion texts offered here can elicit powerful emotions and questions in students. The Holocaust itself raises questions of faith, doubt, and meaning, not only in survivors but in those who study it—including some students today. While the classroom is usually not the place to offer answers to those questions, students should have an opportunity to reflect and process, perhaps using journals.

The strategies for processing emotionally powerful material described on page 3 are a useful resource here. If your class explored Samuel Bak's artwork, the Color, Symbol, Image teaching strategy can be an especially relevant and meaningful way to synthesize ideas and reflect on this section of the memoir.

Faith after the Holocaust

David Weiss Halivni is a Jewish theologian and Holocaust survivor. Like Elie Wiesel, he was born in Sighet and was deported to Auschwitz with his family. From a young age, Halivni was a person of deep faith, and he had devoted his early life to the study of religious texts. As a prisoner at Auschwitz and in slave labor camps, Halivni had no access to books, but he studied portions of the scriptures and other texts that he had memorized and even taught them to others. In his memoir *The Book and the Sword*, Halivni describes coming across a page from a beloved Jewish legal text in an unlikely place: a guard in the slave labor camp had used it as a wrapper for a sandwich, his evening snack.

> His sandwich was wrapped in a page of *Orach Chaim*, a volume of the *Shulchan Aruch*, Pesil Balaban's edition . . . As a child of a poor but scholarly home, I had always wanted to have her edition . . . Here, of all places, in the shadows of the tunnel, under the threatening gaze of the German, a page of the *Shulchan Aruch* . . . met my eyes . . .
>
> Upon seeing this wrapper, I instinctively fell at the feet of the guard, without even realizing why; the mere letters propelled me. With tears in my eyes I implored him to give me this *bletl*, this page. For a while he didn't know what was happening; he thought I was suffering from epilepsy. He immediately put his hand to his revolver, the usual reaction to an unknown situation. But then he understood. This was, I explained to him, a page from a book I had studied at home. Please, I sobbed, give it to me as a souvenir. He gave me the bletl and I took it back to the camp. On the Sundays we had off, we now had not only Oral Torah but Written Torah as well. The bletl became a visible symbol of the connection between the camp and the activities of Jews throughout history.[1]

Later in his memoir, Halivni discusses how the war and the Holocaust influenced his religious life:

> I remember, after I came to the United States, Moshe Meisels Amishai, the Hebrew philosopher, asked me, speaking in Yiddish, "Were you religious before the war?" and I said, "Yes, of course, I was a chasid." "Are you religious now?" he asked. I said, "Yes." And he said, "I understand those who were religious before and became irreligious after, and those who were irreligious before and became religious after. I can't understand those who were religious before and remained religious after. *Nothing happened?* Something must have changed." . . .
>
> Opposite forces bear upon the survivor. On the one hand, one must find fault with what happened, for if there is no fault, there is indirect affirmation. If you continue doing now what you would have done before, then you are saying that nothing was wrong, that you do not relate to what happened . . . On the other hand, if you acknowledge the wrong, then you risk cutting off the branch upon which you rest. . . .
>
> We must somehow find room for acknowledging that something went awfully wrong—that nobody extended help, not even God himself . . . Nonetheless, as religious Jews, we have to know that without God there is no humanity. Life makes sense only if we are hooked into something higher, something transcendent. It's

---

[1] David Weiss Halivni, *The Book and the Sword: A Life of Learning in the Shadow of Destruction* (Boulder, CO: Westview Press, 1998), 68–69.

like a trolley car, if you've ever been in a trolley car: you think the conductor's in charge, but the power comes from above. "Walk humbly with the Lord thy God" (Micah 6:8)—like a child holding hands. *You must hold hands, and walk.* But that does not mean that you always have to say, particularly in remembrance of the Holocaust, "What you did was right." It was terribly wrong.[1]

---

[1] Ibid., 161–62, 164.

Quotations about Michelangelo's and Bak's Work

Artist Samuel Bak creates paintings influenced by his experience of surviving the Holocaust as a child in the Vilna ghetto. In the painting *Creation of War Time*, he in part recasts the relationship between God and humans depicted in Michelangelo's *Creation of Adam*.

Scholar Lawrence Langer writes of Michelangelo's *Creation of Adam*:

> Michelangelo's "Creation of Adam" is charged with tension between human expectation and divine wish. The focal point is the narrow space dividing God's resolute finger from Adam's languid hand, awaiting the spark of vitality that will give it life. The symmetrical skill that separates God in a regal purple cloak from a naked Adam highlights the one-way transmission of energy from omnipotent divine source to inert human dependent.

Langer writes of Bak's painting:

> "Creation of War Time" repeats the confrontation between Adam and God, but here God is even less defined, a cutout from the empty space that surrounds His image. A helmeted Adam leans upon a landscape in ruins, the tatters of his rainbow-colored garments summoning up memories of an ancient broken promise from biblical times. In the distance rise the familiar ominous pillars of smoke, haunting the foreground with their annihilation, while just behind them the curved tops of the Tablets of the Law peek furtively over a low ridge of stone. What fresh covenant will spring from the ravages of war and the Holocaust? The sole sign of renewal is the tree that emerges from the silhouette of God's forearm. But the wary spectator will also note that it is adjacent to His hand, nailed to the wall while blood drips from a different kind of stigmata, leaving us with the disturbing facsimile of a wounded God. Both the painting and its images are inspired by times of violence that form a major legacy to the modern mind. Any renewal or return to creative vigor must be born from arduous passage through Bak's fragmented landscapes of devastation.[1]

---

1 Lawrence L. Langer, *In a Different Light: The Book of Genesis in the Art of Samuel Bak* (Boston: Pucker Art Publications, 2001), 6, 9.

Creation of War Time, Samuel Bak

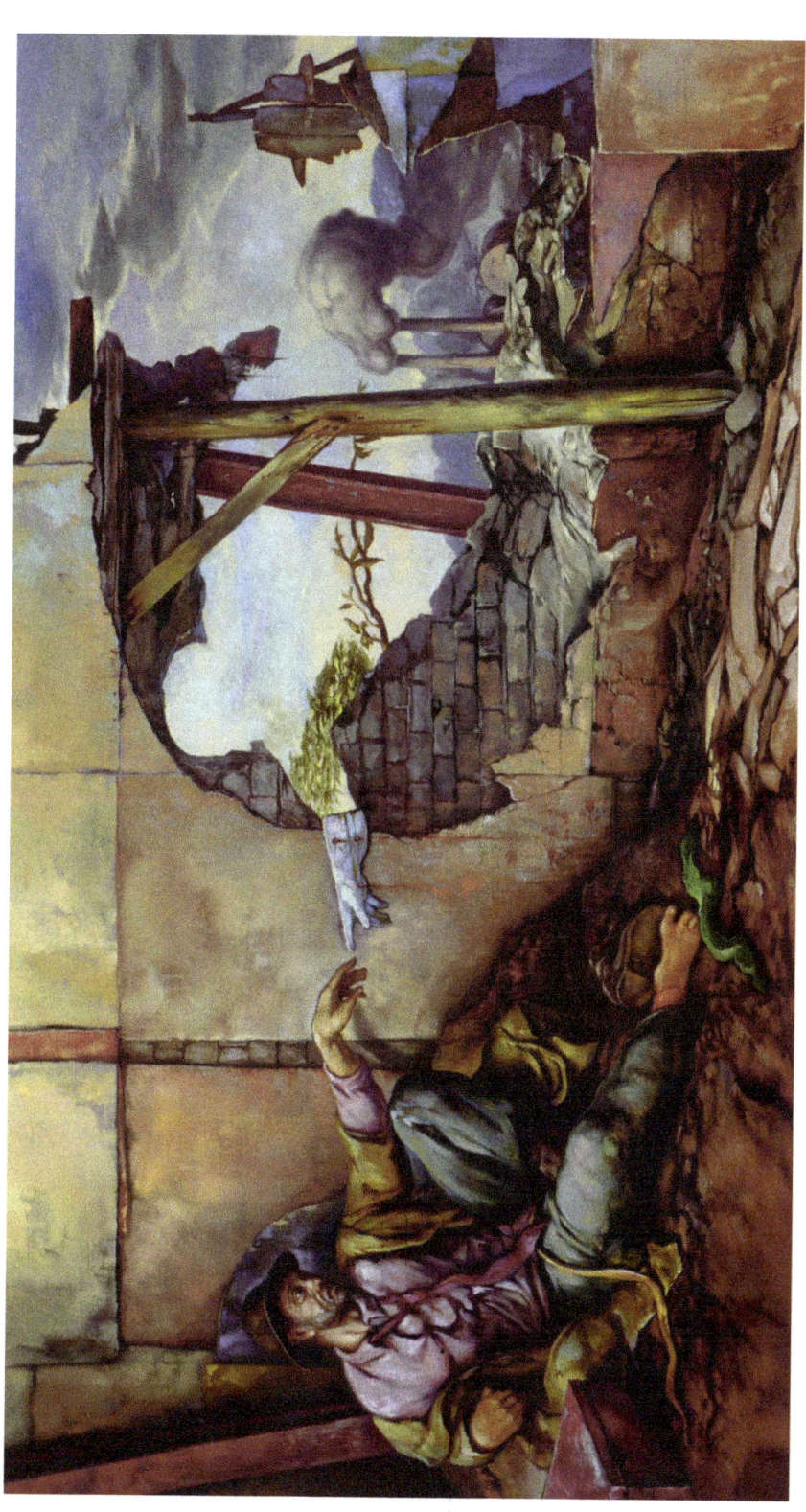

Artist and Holocaust survivor Samuel Bak's 1999 painting depicts the relationship between God and human.

Courtesy of the Pucker Gallery

Creation of Adam, Michelangelo

Michelangelo painted a series of frescoes portraying biblical characters and stories on the ceiling of the Sistine Chapel, c. 1508–1512.

Courtesy of Erich Lessing/Art Resource, NY

SECTION 7

FINAL DAYS

Reading Assignment

Pages 85–112

Overview

The last section of *Night* tells the story of the final days of the Holocaust for Eliezer and his father. After leaving Buna, they march 42 miles through the ice and snow. They were among thousands of prisoners forced on "death marches" from Poland, as German authorities tried to hide evidence of their crimes from approaching Allied forces. Thousands walked from Poland to camps within occupied Germany, and thousands died along the way.

Eliezer and his father survive the march to a new camp, Gleiwitz. There, unable to sleep, Eliezer spends the night listening to the sound of a violin playing to an audience of dead and dying men. The violinist is Juliek, a fellow prisoner from Buna. The next morning, he too is dead. Three days later, the prisoners, still without food or drink, face yet another "selection." Once again, Eliezer's father is "selected," but in the confusion, the two end up on the train to yet another camp, a desperate journey that kills many of the prisoners.

When the train finally reaches Buchenwald, a concentration camp in Germany, only 12 prisoners in Eliezer's car are still alive. Eliezer desperately tries to protect his sick father, but the next day, his father is dead. Eliezer is unable to cry and even admits that in "the recesses of his weakened conscience" he now feels free.

Three months later, as the war is drawing to a close, the Germans decide to evacuate the camp and kill off the remaining prisoners. Before they can act, the camp resistance movement drives the Germans out of Buchenwald. That evening the Americans arrive. The book ends with Eliezer in the hospital, a victim of food poisoning. After hovering between life and death for two weeks, he looks into a mirror, the first he has seen in a year. He sees a "corpse" gazing back from the mirror: "The look in his eyes as he gazed at me has never left me" (page 115).

> **Locate Gleiwitz and Buchenwald on the map "Eliezer's Forced Journey."**

Exploring the Text

Ask students for their questions or comments about what they have read in this section. Then use the following questions as journal or discussion prompts to guide students' exploration of the text.

1. After the forced march, the prisoners are crammed into a barracks. That night, Juliek plays a fragment of a Beethoven concerto on a violin, which he has managed to keep the entire time he was at Auschwitz. What do you think prompts

Juliek to play that evening? What does the music mean to Eliezer? What does it mean to the other prisoners who hear it? To Juliek?

Record an event on your identity timeline.

2. How does Wiesel write about his body in this section of the memoir? What quotations help you understand the connection between his body and his identity? Add these quotations to your identity timeline for Eliezer.

3. As the train filled with prisoners passes through German towns, a worker throws a piece of bread into the wagon and the prisoners fight violently for it. Wiesel briefly interrupts his narrative to tell a story from another time, long after the war, about a woman throwing coins to poor children in Aden, Yemen. Why does he tell this story? How does this recollection affect you as a reader?

4. In this section, Eliezer tells of three fathers and three sons: Rabbi Eliahu and his son, the father whose son killed him for a piece of bread, and finally his own father and himself. What words does Eliezer use to describe his response to each of the first two stories? What do the three stories have in common? How do they differ?

5. What mix of emotions does Eliezer feel after his father's death? What does Eliezer mean when he writes that he feels "free at last"?

6. This section of the text is filled with images of movement. Wiesel describes the marches and the trains and also uses language of movement in other ways: a distraught man "had reached the end" (page 102); in the wagon, "All boundaries had been crossed" (page 103). What other examples of movement metaphors can you find? What does all this movement mean to the prisoners? What does it signify for readers? What kinds of "journeys" have Eliezer and the others experienced?

7. Wiesel names just a few specific dates in the whole of his memoir, all in this last section of the book: January 28 and January 29, 1945, and April 5, 10, and 11. Why does he give a more precise accounting of time here? Why do you think he marks these dates specifically?

8. At the end of the book, Eliezer says that when he looks into a mirror for the first time in a year, he sees a "corpse" looking back. He ends the book by stating, "The look in his eyes as he gazed at me has never left me." What does that sentence mean?

9. Now that you have finished the memoir, why do you think Wiesel gave it the title *Night*? What did the word *night* mean to you before you read the book? What does the word *night* symbolize for you now that you have read Wiesel's story? What might the title imply about how Wiesel's story continues after the conclusion of this book?

Connecting to the Central Question

After exploring the text and reviewing the events that take place in this section of the book, give students an opportunity to revisit their thinking about this guide's central question:

Q: *How is our identity shaped and reshaped by the circumstances we encounter? How do tragedy and trauma influence an individual's identity and choices?*

Give students a few minutes to reflect and write in their journals about the changes they have noticed in Eliezer's identity as he endures forced marches, loses his father, and barely survives after the end of the war. If you are having students use identity timelines, they may help in this reflection. Do the students' observations about Eliezer's changing identity support their previous thinking about the central question? Or do they prompt them to revise their thinking?

> **Refer to your identity timeline.**

A culminating activity designed to help students synthesize their thinking about the central question over the course of the entire book is provided below (Socratic seminar).

Activities for Deeper Understanding

1. Socratic Seminar

Our reading of *Night* has focused in large part on the theme of identity and on this central question:

Q: *How is our identity shaped and reshaped by the circumstances we encounter? How do tragedy and trauma shape an individual's identity and choices?*

A "Socratic seminar" gives students the opportunity to synthesize their thinking about the theme of identity, to revisit key moments in the text with the help of their identity timelines, and to practice key reading and discussion skills. It can also support students in developing their ideas prior to writing an essay. Refer to the instructions below and to the Socratic Seminar teaching strategy to plan and facilitate this activity with your students.

Preparation

In class: If you have never held a Socratic seminar with your students, spend a few moments brainstorming the qualities that make for a successful seminar. These might include defining norms for respectful dialogue, grounding discussion with evidence from the text, asking probing questions, and sharing airtime. You can also use these criteria to create a grading rubric to evaluate the seminar and students' participation.

At home: Remind students of the central question and explain that the Socratic seminar will explore these questions through the lens of *Night*. To prepare for the seminar, students should:

- Select three to five key moments and quotations that speak to the central question. If students created identity timelines for Eliezer, they can draw on their timelines for relevant events and quotations. Otherwise, stu-

Record an event on your identity timeline.

dents can use their notes and review the memoir itself to prepare. They should come to class with these quotations marked in their books and with notes about how each quotation connects to the central question.

- Write an initial response to the central question in their journals, with the quotations and notes they selected in mind. The goal of this writing is to help students develop their thinking, not to create a final product.

Implementation

Depending on the number of students in your class, consider breaking them into smaller groups so that each student can more readily participate in the discussion. On the day of the Socratic seminar, try to arrange the classroom desks in circles or horseshoes so that the students in each group can see or hear each other. There should be no back rows.

Before beginning, check to make sure that students have completed their preparation work and remind them of the rubric or ground rules.

A Socratic seminar conversation should be guided primarily by students. Begin with one part of the central question. As the discussion progresses, students can also introduce other questions of their own. Socratic seminars should be held for at least 20 minutes and can last for a whole class period or even longer.

Reflection

A few minutes before the end of class, ask students to write in their journals about new insights or ideas that surfaced during the seminar; they can also freewrite about one part of the central question. Alternatively, students can reflect on the process of the Socratic seminar: What went well? What was challenging? What role did they themselves play in the discussion? What would they like to do differently in a future Socratic seminar?

Extension

Students can use their preparation for the seminar and the ideas generated in the seminar itself to inform an essay written in response to one part of the central question.

2. Reflect on Memory, Loss, and the Power of Art

This section of *Night* includes the poignant story of Juliek, the Polish prisoner who has somehow kept his violin with him in camp. As the starving and exhausted prisoners collapse after their arrival at Gleiwitz, Juliek plays part of Beethoven's violin concerto in "a concert given before the dead and dying." Eliezer says, "Never before had I heard such a beautiful sound . . . He was playing his life. His whole being was gliding over the strings" (page 95).

Hungarian poet Miklós Radnóti also evoked memories of life and beauty in a poem now known as "Forced March," written during his evacuation from a forced labor camp in 1944. Distribute copies of **Forced March** and discuss the following questions:

- What memories does Radnóti describe? What sights, sounds, smells, and feelings does he evoke?

- How does the structure and appearance of the poem on the page reinforce its themes?

- What does the poem have in common with Wiesel's passage about Juliek?

- What might the writing of the poem and the playing of the violin have meant for each man?

After your discussion, you might choose to play a recording of the Beethoven violin concerto. As students listen, they can write in their journals, compose a poem, or draw a picture. In writing or images, students can capture what mood the music evokes, how it adds to their understanding of this scene in *Night*, and what emotions it arouses in them.

3. Examine the Meaning of "Freedom" after Liberation

Night ends as Buchenwald is liberated by American forces. Yet Elie Wiesel's story, like that of all survivors, did not end with the liberation of the camps and the end of the war. Two of the resources in this section, the video testimony of American soldier Leon Bass and the reading After Liberation, paint a picture of the ongoing struggles facing survivors.

Distribute and read After Liberation and watch Leon Bass's testimony, Eyewitness to Buchenwald (see hstry.is/TeachingNight). Use these questions for discussion:

- How do these sources describe the physical, mental, and emotional state of survivors?

- What questions and choices did survivors face after liberation? What options did Wiesel and others consider?

- What did "liberation" mean for Wiesel? To what extent were survivors "free" after they were released from the camps?

- What do you think Wiesel meant by "the other side of the wall" in his letter to Judith Hemmendinger? What was the wall that separated the survivors from her and others who tried to help them? What do you think allowed some survivors to cross to the other side of that wall?

Forced March

Hungarian Jewish poet Miklós Radnóti wrote poems during his imprisonment and evacuation from a forced labor camp in Yugoslavia. He was fatally shot during a death march in November 1944 and buried in a mass grave. When the grave was exhumed months later, several poems were discovered in his clothing, including one now known as "Forced March."

A fool he is who, collapsed,   rises and walks again,
Ankles and knees moving   alone, like wandering pain,
Yet he, as if wings uplifted him,   sets out on his way,
And in vain the ditch calls him   back, who dare not stay.
And if asked why not, he might answer   — without leaving his path —
That his wife was awaiting him,   and a saner, more beautiful death.
Poor fool! He's out of his mind: now, for a long time,
Only scorched winds have whirled   over the houses at home,
The wall has been laid low,   the plum-tree is broken there,
The night of our native hearth   flutters, thick with fear.
Oh if only I could believe   that everything of worth
Were not just in my heart —   that I still had home on earth;
If only I had! As before,   jam made fresh from the plum
Would cool on the old verandah,   in peace the bee would hum
And an end-of-summer stillness   would bask in the drowsy garden,
Naked among the leaves   would sway the fruit-trees' burden,
And Fanni would be waiting,   blonde, by russet hedgerow,
As the slow morning painted   slow shadow over shadow —
Could it perhaps still be?   The moon tonight's so round!
Don't leave me friend, shout at me: I'll get up off the ground![1]

---

[1] Miklós Radnóti, *Forced March: Selected Poems,* trans. Clive Wilmer and George Gömöri, rev. ed. (London: Enitharmon, 2003), 85.

After Liberation

Although Elie Wiesel ends *Night* immediately after the liberation of Buchenwald, his story—and his struggle to return to life—would continue. Years later, Wiesel wrote at greater length about his memories of liberation:

> Strangely, we did not "feel" the victory. There were no joyous embraces, no shouts or songs to mark our happiness, for that word was meaningless to us. We were not happy. We wondered whether we ever would be. . . .
>
> I spent several days in the hospital (the former SS hospital) in a semiconscious state. When I was discharged, I felt drained. It took all my mental resources to figure out where I was. I knew my father was dead. My mother was probably dead, since Mengele would have considered her too old to work. Likewise my grandmother. My little sister was too little. I hoped Bea and Hilda might still be alive, but could I find out? Lists were being circulated. Racked with anxiety, I devoured them. I found nothing but was told not to lose heart: other lists were being drawn up. They came, and I leapt upon them. Still there was nothing. Here and there my eyes fell upon a Wiesel, but no Bea or Hilda. Feig, Deutsch, Hollander, Slomowics—some names of cousins were there, thank God. But where were Bea and Hilda? Each list carved a deeper void within me. I was free, but I was more distraught than ever.[1]

Wiesel was one of hundreds of children among the survivors at Buchenwald. Many were orphans. They debated what to do. Eventually, a group of boys from Buchenwald was invited to go to a home for orphans in Écouis, France, run by a child welfare organization. Judith Feist Hemmendinger was a volunteer who offered to help care for the children. When the overwhelmed director of the home quit his job shortly after the boys arrived, she took his place and remained with the boys until September 1947, when the last boy was placed in a permanent home. She wrote of her experiences:

> Écouis was an abandoned sanatorium placed at the disposal of the OSE [a group that saved Jewish children during the war] by the French government. The OSE had prepared 500 beds for little children, unaware that nearly 400 were aged twelve to twenty-one and only thirty were between eight and twelve years old. They looked like bandits, suspicious and mute. Their heads were shorn; all dressed the same, with faces still swollen from hunger and not a smile to be seen. Their eyes bespoke sadness and suspicion. They were apathetic towards the outside world. They likened the supervisors to guards and were terror stricken at the sight of doctors who reminded them of Mengele, the man who, upon their arrival in Auschwitz, had sent the weak ones to gas chambers, the able-bodied to slave labor . . .
>
> For these young people, all adults were potential enemies who were not to be trusted. One day they were served Camembert cheese for dessert. The strong smell convinced them that it was poison. They threw the cheese at the adults who were supervising dinner. . . .
>
> There were many visitors who came to Écouis to talk with the young survivors of Buchenwald. There were journalists and rabbis and numerous officials who came to meet with these earliest arrivals from Germany . . . The children listened silently to the beautiful and affectionate words, noted that it was well meant, but did not react for they were totally disillusioned about human nature.

---

[1] Elie Wiesel, *All Rivers Run to the Sea: Memoirs* (New York: Knopf, 1995), 95–98.

One day Chaplain [Robert] Marcus of the American army came to Écouis. He had met the boys before in Buchenwald. They sat in a circle around him on the lawn. The Chaplain stood in front of them unable to utter a word, overcome by his emotions, tears streamed down his cheeks. It had been a long time since the children had seen an adult cry. Something in them thawed and they too began to cry. One of them described later, "The Chaplain returned to us our souls. He reawakened the feeling we had buried within us."[2]

Not long after Hemmendinger's account was published in 1989, she received a letter from one of the "boys," Elie Wiesel:

I read your book and I remember. I see us back in 1945. . . . The dumbfounded instructors, the disoriented children . . . Did you know, Judith, that we pitied you? We felt sorry for you. I hope you are not angry that I speak so openly? You thought you could educate us, and yet the younger of us knew more than the oldest of you, about what existed in the world, of the futility of life, the brutal triumph of death. We were not impressed with your age, or your authority. We observed you with amusement and mistrust. We felt ourselves stronger than you. How did you succeed to tame us, Judith? . . .

Reasonably, Judith, we were doomed to live cloistered lives on the other side of the wall. And yet we succeeded in a short time to find ourselves on the same side. To whom can we attribute the miracle? How can one explain it? To our belief? To yours?[3]

---

2 Judith Hemmendinger, "The Buchenwald Boys," in Judith Hemmendinger and Robert Krell, *The Children of Buchenwald: Child Survivors of the Holocaust and Their Post-War Lives* (Gefen Press, 2000), 27–31.
3 Elie Wiesel, quoted in Hemmendinger and Krell, *The Children of Buchenwald*, 10–11.

SECTION 8

Post-Reading: MEMORY AND RESPONSIBILITY

Overview

In 1986, Elie Wiesel reflected,

> I remember: it happened yesterday or eternities ago. A young Jewish boy discovered the kingdom of night. I remember his bewilderment, I remember his anguish. It all happened so fast. The ghetto. The deportation. The sealed cattle car. The fiery altar upon which the history of our people and the future of mankind were meant to be sacrificed.
>
> I remember: he asked his father: "Can this be true?" This is the twentieth century, not the Middle Ages. Who would allow such crimes to be committed? How could the world remain silent?
>
> And now the boy is turning to me: "Tell me," he asks. "What have you done with my future? What have you done with your life?"[1]

In the 71 years between liberation and his death in 2016, Wiesel wrote, taught, and became known as a witness to the Holocaust and a prominent voice of conscience. After the war, he learned that his mother and youngest sister perished at Auschwitz, but his two older sisters survived. He worked in France and Israel as a teacher, translator, and journalist, but he didn't begin writing the book that would become *Night* until 1955, fully ten years after liberation; it was published in 1960. He later emigrated to the United States and wrote dozens of books, works of fiction, essays, and even music. He urged leaders to respond to injustice around the world, speaking out about the plight of Jews in the then–Soviet Union and Iran, against massacres in Bosnia, and in favor of peace and human dignity around the world. In 1986, he was awarded the Nobel Peace Prize. *Night* became a standard text in high schools and colleges, selling hundreds of thousands of copies each year.

To Wiesel, the memory and legacy of the Holocaust created a profound sense of responsibility to be a witness to suffering and inhumanity in our contemporary world. The activities and resources in this section explore what it means to be a witness and how our memory of history might influence our choices in the world today.

---

[1] From Elie Wiesel's 1986 Nobel Peace Prize acceptance speech.

Activities for Deeper Understanding

1. Journal Reflection

If you have been using journals with your class, students will likely have written many entries by the time they finish reading the memoir. This activity invites students to reread their journal entries, notice patterns and growth, and reflect on their learning in a final journal entry.

a. Begin with a conversation that reviews some of the themes the class has explored while reading *Night*. You can elicit these themes from students or name some that were most important, like identity, family, faith, suffering, choices, and responsibility.

b. Ask students to return to their journals and read their entries from beginning to end. Using self-stick notes or a highlighter, students should select three moments in their journals that stand out to them in some way: an entry where they arrived at a new insight about one of the themes of the novel, an entry that explored a question the student is still thinking about, and an entry that they would want to change because their thinking has shifted.

c. Ask students to write a new journal entry in which they look back on their learning over the course of studying *Night*. What new insights and understandings have they gained about the memoir, about the Holocaust, or about universal human themes? What questions do they still have? How has reading about someone else's experience changed them and the way they think about their own lives? You can also ask students to begin this journal entry by completing this sentence stem: "I used to think _____. Now I think _____ because _____."

2. What Does It Mean to Be a Witness?

When Elie Wiesel told the story of his experiences during the Holocaust, he often insisted to audiences that "to listen to a witness is to become a witness."[2] Wiesel emphasized that the Holocaust was not only a historical event but a call to conscience for people everywhere. Even as he resisted easy "lessons" drawn from the traumatic history he survived, he argued that the memory of the Holocaust was essential to building a more just and peaceful world.

This activity asks students to engage with one or more readings and videos to explore the connection between being a witness to history and developing a sense of moral responsibility. These resources include Forgetting Isn't Healing, a reading about Wiesel's role as a voice of conscience after the Holocaust; Benjamin Ferencz: Watcher of the Sky (see hstry.is/TeachingNight), a short video excerpt about Nazi war crimes prosecutor and activist Benjamin Ferencz; and the reading The Holocaust as a Call to Conscience, a personal essay by a journalist and former student of Wiesel's, Sonari Glinton.

Teachers can ask students to engage with one or more of these sources and then lead a discussion using some of the questions below to explore the connection between

---

[2] Quoted in Paul Vitello, "The Urgency of Bearing Witness," *New York Times*, April 9, 2010, www.nytimes.com/2010/04/10/nyregion/10calligrapher.html.

memory, witness, and responsibility. (Alternatively, teachers can use the Big Paper teaching strategy to engage students in a silent discussion on questions 4 and/or 5.)

1. How did Wiesel and Ferencz connect their memories of the war and the Holocaust to the choices they made during the remainder of their lives? How do you think their personal histories shaped their universes of obligation?

2. Unlike Wiesel and Ferencz, Sonari Glinton did not have a direct experience of the war or the Holocaust. In what sense is he a witness? How does Glinton connect Wiesel's teachings to his own life experiences as a black man in the United States?

3. What responsibility do witnesses have? What phrases or sentences in the readings or film reveal something about what it might mean to be a witness?

4. Do you agree with Elie Wiesel that "to listen to a witness is to become a witness"? In what sense are you a witness now that you have read his memoir? Is there something in your own world or life experience that you feel a responsibility to remember and share with others?

5. How has studying the history of the Holocaust and Wiesel's story informed your own sense of responsibility today?

3. Memory and Art

Elie Wiesel once said, "[I]f anything can, it is memory that will save humanity. For me, hope without memory is like memory without hope." As students conclude their study of *Night*, this activity prompts them to reflect on their learning, consider what they want to remember, and create a piece of artwork to help them hold on to those key ideas and insights.

a. First, share Wiesel's quote "[I]f anything can, it is memory that will save humanity. For me, hope without memory is like memory without hope," and discuss it with students. Why does Wiesel say that memory will save humanity? What is the connection between memory and hope? Why is it important to have both memory and hope as we try to solve the problems in our world?

b. Next, ask students to write in their journals or discuss in pairs: What have you learned through studying *Night* that feels most relevant and essential to you personally and to our world today? What ideas, insights, feelings, and questions do you want to be sure to hold on to? What do you most want to remember? (If students already completed the journal reflection activity suggested in this section, they can draw on those ideas and will likely not need as much time to write.)

c. Ask students to create a work of art that will help them remember. Memorials, of course, are one form of art whose purpose is to keep memory alive, and students can design a memorial to reflect what they learned from Wiesel's story. They can also create a drawing, painting, or collage or write a poem. Whatever they create should communicate something important that they learned in their study of *Night*.

d. As a final step, you can display the artwork in the classroom and give students time to view and respond to their classmates' work.

Forgetting Isn't Healing

Sonari Glinton is a journalist who read *Night* as a young boy and went on to study with Elie Wiesel when he was a student at Boston University. In a 2016 essay, Glinton describes how he was first drawn to *Night* simply because it looked like a quick read for a book report he'd been assigned to write. He was surprised to discover that he identified with its protagonist, even though, as a black boy growing up in Chicago, he and Eliezer would seem to have little in common. Still, Glinton saw himself in Eliezer's love of books and theology and his status as part of an out-group in his society. Eliezer's sense of fragility and vulnerability felt familiar.

Years later, while at Boston University, Glinton was selected to be a student in one of Elie Wiesel's courses on literature and memory. Each student had to present a book to the class, and Glinton chose *The Bluest Eye*, a novel by Toni Morrison that so resonated with his own experiences as a black man that he broke down in tears during the class discussion. Later, he apologized to Wiesel and vowed to "get past" his feelings about race. In an essay written just after Wiesel's death in 2016, Glinton recalls,

> I remember him leaning in and asking why I would want to forget.
>
> Memory, he said, wasn't just for Holocaust survivors. The people who ask us to forget are not our friends. Memory not only honors those we lost but also gives us strength. In those office hours, he gave me a shield, practical words and thoughts that would help me—a gay, Nigerian, Catholic journalist. He gave me tools that would aid me in an often hostile world. Over the years, I have found myself quoting Professor Wiesel to white people who want me to "get over race." *"That's old." "It was a hundred years ago."* But Professor Wiesel had been emphatic: Nothing good comes of forgetting; remember, so that my past doesn't become your future . . .
>
> So, as a journalist, at times without noticing, I find myself helping others to remember or bear witness. I will not forget the victims of police torture I reported on in Chicago, or Lafonso Rollins, who was falsely imprisoned for rape . . . And when Trayvon Martin's parents went to Capitol Hill and the press corps was less than sensitive, I remember kneeling in front of his grieving parents with my microphone. Why in those moments would I want to forget?
>
> In my personal life, though, remembering—and making others remember—the unfairness of racism is a harder choice. I am NPR's car reporter. For a normal gay man, being a car reporter and living near Beverly Hills should be a dream come true. I am a black man. That means that driving exotic cars or testing cars can be dangerous. I have been stopped at least five times this year . . .
>
> During the 2012 presidential campaign, I was stopped in Michigan, Indiana, Iowa and Ohio. I have tried to shield my friends and co-workers from the fear, anger and indignities I face on a daily basis. That futile exercise has cost me dearly. I realize that I have a responsibility to let people know about what affects me. But I also know that, as a black man, that has costs as well. Mentioning race to white Americans has almost never failed to cause me pain or to be attacked . . . As I grow older, and feel the need to speak up more, I understand just a little the burden Elie Wiesel took on.

And that's what I mourn when I think about him now. I mourn the man who taught me that in many ways laughter is the greatest victory. I mourn the man who saw me struggling and tried to give me tools to survive. I mourn the man who let me know that those who demand that I forget are not my friends. I mourn the teacher who made a solemn vow to me as a student in the '90s and kept it. I mourn the fact that with him gone, I'm now more responsible for bearing witness. It saddens me that there's still so much to bear witness to.[1]

---

[1] Sonari Glinton, "Forgetting Isn't Healing: Lessons from Elie Wiesel," *Code Switch*, NPR website, July 14, 2016, www.npr.org/sections/codeswitch/2016/07/14/484558040/forgetting-isnt-healing-lessons-from-elie-wiesel.

The Holocaust as a Call to Conscience

The legacy and memory of the Holocaust remain alive in numerous people, places, and institutions today. The history lives in international bodies like the United Nations and the International Criminal Court, in the stories of survivors and their families, and in the sites and memorials that millions of people visit each year. One of the most important legacies of the Holocaust, though, isn't a physical person, place, or thing. It is an idea, a promise most often expressed in the phrase "never again."

Elie Wiesel urged his readers and listeners to see the Holocaust not just as a historical event but as a call to conscience for people everywhere. He linked world leaders' failures to stop Nazi crimes in the 1930s and 1940s with the problem of indifference in the twenty-first century. When the United States Holocaust Memorial Museum opened in 1993, Wiesel spoke at the dedication to an audience that included then president Bill Clinton. At the time, the country of Yugoslavia had broken apart and was at war, and a violent campaign of "ethnic cleansing" against minorities was underway there. Wiesel's remarks made a bridge between his life history and the present world. He told his audience,

> [A]s you walk through those exhibits, looking into the eyes of the killers and their victims, ask yourselves how could murderers do what they did and go on living? Why was Berlin encouraged in its belief that it could decree with impunity the humiliation, persecution, extermination of an entire people? Why weren't the railways leading to Birkenau bombed by Allied bombers? As long as I live I will not understand that. And why was there no public outcry of indignation and outrage? . . .
>
> Oh, I don't believe there are answers. There are no answers. And this museum is not an answer; it is a question mark. If there is a response, it is a response in responsibility . . .
>
> What have we learned? We have learned some lessons, minor lessons, perhaps, that we are all responsible, and indifference is a sin and a punishment. And we have learned that when people suffer we cannot remain indifferent.
>
> And, Mr. President, I cannot not tell you something. I have been in the former Yugoslavia last fall. I cannot sleep since for what I have seen. As a Jew I am saying that we must do something to stop the bloodshed in that country! People fight each other and children die. Why? Something, anything must be done.
>
> This is a lesson. There are many other lessons. You will come, you will learn. We shall learn together.

Wiesel's message continues to resonate in the twenty-first century, at a time when many would say that the "lessons" of the Holocaust have not been learned and the promise of "never again" has not been fulfilled. Remembering post–World War II genocides in Cambodia, Rwanda, the former Yugoslavia, and Darfur, a group of scholars and activists observed, "Leaders at every level seem to love hearing themselves declare 'Never Again.' But those who mean it have no power and those with power never mean it. The record speaks for itself . . ."

In the face of this dismal record, the memory of the Holocaust continues to inspire people to work to end genocide and mass violence—a task that will require the dedication, persistence, and vigilance of generations.

NIGHT Glossary Terms

Antisemitism: A form of racism, hostility, and discrimination toward Jewish people as a group.

Appelplatz: German word referring to the area in concentration camps where prisoners were required to assemble for daily roll call. These spaces were also often used for humiliation and execution of prisoners.

Aryan: Refers to a mythical race of people that many Northern Europeans believed they had descended from and that was described by the Nazis as the "master race." The myth of the Aryan race was used to justify discrimination against and persecution of peoples that the Nazis considered to be of inferior, non-Aryan races.

Auschwitz: A network of camps, including multiple forced labor camps and a killing center (Auschwitz-Birkenau) equipped with gas chambers. More than one million people, mostly Jewish, were murdered by the Nazis there.

Babylon: A major city in ancient Mesopotamia, located in present-day Iraq, near the modern city of Hillah. In 587 BCE, Babylonian general Nebuchadnezzar destroyed the city of Jerusalem and the Hebrew temple there. As a result, Babylon often symbolizes brutal oppression in Jewish and Christian tradition.

Barracks: A building or group of buildings in which laborers or prisoners are housed, often in wretched conditions. During the Holocaust, prisoners in the Nazi camp system slept in barracks.

Beadle: An official at a church or synagogue who assists in religious functions and is the caretaker of the building.

Blockälteste: A German word that translates to "block elder." This person was a *kapo* who was in charge of the other inmates in a single barrack in a Nazi camp. See *kapo*.

Buchenwald: One of the largest concentration camps used by the Nazis during the Holocaust. While Buchenwald did not have gas chambers, many died there due to malnourishment, disease, hard labor, medical experimentation, shooting, or hanging. Further, many Soviet prisoners of war were brought to Buchenwald for execution.

Chasid: A member of a sect of Judaism that focuses on spirituality, piety, and traditionalism. Hasidism still exists today, with many Hasidic Jews living in close-knit "courts" in America, Britain, and Israel. These communities each follow a specific "rebbe," or rabbi, often from a dynastic line of rabbis.

Chief Rabbi: The title given to the religious leader of a given country's Jewish community.

Communism: A political and economic ideology based on the ideas of Karl Marx and Friedrich Engels, in which property is owned collectively and distributed to citizens according to need. A version of the ideology was the foundation for the government of the Soviet Union, and many countries had communist political groups in the twentieth century.

Concentration camp: A camp used to detain large numbers of prisoners, usually in harsh conditions and without legal rights. The Nazis initially established concentration camps to imprison and torture political opponents. Eventually they also used the camps to imprison Jews, Roma and Sinti, prisoners of war, and other groups they desired to remove from German society. Prisoners in Nazi camps were intentionally malnourished and often forced to perform hard labor, leading to frequent deaths. During World War II, Nazi concentration camps increasingly became sites for executions and mass murder.

Conflagration: A large fire that destroys a lot of land or property.

Convalescent: Someone who is recovering from an illness or period of poor health.

Crematoria: Factory-like buildings containing large furnaces located in Nazi concentration camps and killing centers in which the corpses of those killed were burned.

Death camp: A camp constructed by the Nazis solely for the purpose of mass murder in gas chambers and the cremation and disposal of corpses. Also known as a killing center.

Delousing: To kill lice or other parasitic insects during the process of cleaning someone. During the Holocaust, this was the pretext that Nazi physicians used to deceive people into entering gas chambers.

Dysentery: A potentially fatal infection of the intestines, which is characterized by bloody diarrhea. It is most often contracted by drinking contaminated water.

Emigration certificates: Certain documentation required for a citizen to move out of a country, and later into another. These certificates were increasingly difficult for Jews in German-occupied territories to obtain during World War II.

Expulsion: The forcing of someone to leave a place. In the context of the Holocaust, many Jews were expelled from their homes and towns and forced into camps.

Fascism: A political ideology that professes the necessity for the absolute unity of the population behind a single charismatic leader and the supremacy of the good of the nation over the rights of individuals. Hitler and the Nazi Party were influenced by the original fascist movement in Italy in the 1920s.

Foreman: A worker who oversees, supervises, and directs other workers.

Gallows: A typically wooden structure designed specifically for executing people by hanging.

Gestapo: The state secret police in Germany during the Nazi regime, responsible, in part, for rooting out dissenters. Fear induced by the Gestapo caused citizens to inform on friends and neighbors in hopes of protecting themselves from arrest. As secret police, the Gestapo operated with no judicial oversight or accountability. During the Holocaust, the Gestapo also helped the SS deport Jews and run concentration camps.

Ghetto: A specific area or neighborhood of a town in which Jewish homes and businesses were confined.

Gleiwitz: A small German town near the Polish border. Here, the Nazis staged an attack and blamed it on Poland, using the event as an excuse to declare war in September 1939.

Irrevocable: Final; no longer able to be changed.

Jewish Council: Established by the Nazis in Jewish communities and ghettos, these councils were tasked with ensuring that Nazi orders and policies were carried out in their communities. Members of Jewish Councils often faced unthinkable moral dilemmas as they had to decide whether it was in their and their communities' best interests to follow or resist Nazi orders. They were often charged with choosing who would be deported to Nazi camps and killing centers.

Jewish police: Established by the Jewish Councils upon Nazi order, they were tasked with carrying out Nazi directives within the ghetto, including deportations from the ghetto to camps and killing sites. Like Jewish Council members, they were often faced with difficult moral dilemmas.

Kabbalah: Jewish teachings of mysticism.

Kaddish: A hymn of praise to God in the Jewish prayer service said in memorial of someone who has died.

Kapo: Inmates in Nazi camps responsible for supervising other inmates during camp procedures and forced labor. Kapos had some special privileges in the camps, including increased chances of survival, but they were required to enforce brutal Nazi policies and were held responsible for disorder. Some kapos acted, when possible, to protect other inmates from the Nazis. Others treated other inmates savagely.

Kommando: German word for "unit" or "detachment." In Nazi concentration and labor camps, this term was often used to refer to groups of enslaved workers.

Labor camp: Nazi camps in which prisoners were forced to do hard labor, often pointless and humiliating. Many labor camp prisoners died from malnourishment and exhaustion.

Lagerälteste: The highest-ranking kapo in a Nazi concentration or labor camp. He was responsible for overseeing lower-ranking kapos (such as Blockältestes) and making sure rules were followed by prisoners throughout the camp. See *kapo*.

Lament: A passionate expression of grief.

Liquidate: A euphemism the Nazis used for mass murder.

Maimonides: Also known as Moses ben Maimon, a well-known and revered rabbi and physician from medieval Cordova.

Master of the Universe: Term often used in Hebrew prayers to refer to God.

Mengele, Josef: A German SS officer and physician who was in charge of deciding who was fit to work and who would be sent to the gas chambers at Auschwitz. He also performed many deadly human experiments on prisoners.

Messiah: The leader or savior of the Jewish people and prophesied deliverer of the Jewish nation.

Miklós Horthy: Leader of Hungary after World War I and through most of World War II who led a counter-revolution movement called the White Terror to end communism in Hungary. Upon coming to power, he enacted many antisemitic laws, stereotypically associating Jews with communists.

Morale: The amount of confidence and enthusiasm felt by people, often in a stressful or difficult situation.

Oberkapo: A kapo responsible for supervising a labor crew of camp inmates. See *kapo*.

Palestine: A geographical area in the Middle East, situated between Egypt, Syria, and the Arabian Peninsula. This region is the birthplace of Judaism and Christianity and has been fought over and ruled by dozens of kingdoms and empires.

Partisan: A member of an organized body of fighters who attack or harass an enemy, especially behind enemy lines; a guerilla.[1] Between 20,000 and 30,000 Jews fought against the Germans in a variety of partisan groups during World War II. Some of the groups were comprised exclusively of Jews, but most were not. Together, partisan groups were responsible for hindering the Nazis in many ways, including the destruction of armored convoys.

Passover: One of the Jewish religion's most widely celebrated holidays, honoring the story of the Israelites' departure from Egypt.

Rabbinical: Having to do with rabbis or Jewish teachings.

Rebbe: A rabbi or leader of a Hasidic sect.

Red Army: Name given to the Soviet Union's military, due to association between communism and the color red.

Rescinded: Canceled or taken away.

Rosh Hashanah: The Jewish New Year festival.

Sabbath: A day each week set aside for religious observance and rest from work, observed by Jews from Friday evening to Saturday evening and most Christians on Sunday.

Second Front: For much of World War II, the Soviet Union was the only country to be fighting Axis troops in Europe directly, as the western continental Allies such as France, Belgium, the Netherlands, and Luxembourg had since capitulated. With the Allied invasion of Normandy in June of 1944, however, a second line of attack was opened, forcing the Nazi army to split its fighting force in half between the two fronts.

Selection: The process in which a Nazi physician or other official would decide who was fit to work in the camps and who would be sent to the gas chambers to be murdered.

Semite: Historically, anyone who spoke a "semitic language," referring to Arabic and Hebrew. In the nineteenth century, *semite* was used incorrectly to refer to Jews.

Shavuot: A two-day-long Jewish holiday commemorating the day that God gave the Torah to the Israelites.

---

1 From the Jewish Partisan Educational Foundation, www.jewishpartisans.org/t_switch.php?pageName=what+is+what+1.

Shekhinah: The female conjugation of the term for "the Divine presence" in Judaism. Often used to refer to the female aspect of God.

Sonderkommando: Prisoners in killing centers who were forced to lead other prisoners into gas chambers and then, once dead, bring their bodies to the crematoria to be burned. While sonderkommando were temporarily spared from execution, very few survived; the Nazis murdered and replaced the sonderkommando every few months.

Spanish Inquisition: An organization put in place by King Ferdinand II and Queen Isabella I in 1478 to root out Jewish and Muslim influence in Spain through imprisonment, expulsion, or execution.

SS, or Schutzstaffel: Nazi "protection squadrons" that began as bodyguards for Hitler and other party officials in the 1920s and grew into the leading security force, comprised of the supposed "racial elite," in the Nazi government. The SS was responsible for carrying out the "Final Solution to the Jewish Question" and operating Nazi concentration camps and killing centers during World War II.

Synagogue: A building that is the center of Jewish social and spiritual life.

Talmud: The set of teachings on the Torah that form the basis for all Jewish law.

Talmudic treatise: Short essays written after the Talmud was put together that detail some things that the Talmud does not mention. Usually printed at the end of Seder Nezikin in the Talmud.

Temple: Often used synonymously with today's word *synagogue*, *temple* historically referred to the original temple in Jerusalem, before it was destroyed by the Romans in 70 AD.

Transports: Buses and trains used to deliver prisoners to and from Nazi camps.

Yom Kippur: The Day of Atonement, a day when Jewish people repent for their sins and start the year fresh. It is considered the holiest day of the Jewish year.

Zionism: A movement for the re-establishment, development, and protection of a Jewish nation in Israel.

Zionist youth organization: Movements and organizations in Eastern Europe in the twentieth century to help establish a feeling of Jewish nationalism and to keep Zionist ideas alive in Jewish youth.

Zohar: The foundational writing of Kabbalah.

Credits

Excerpt from *All Rivers Run to the Sea: Memoirs* by Elie Wiesel. Reproduced by permission from Penguin Random House and Georges Borchardt, Inc.

Excerpt from "Street for Arrival, Street for Departure" by Charlotte Delbo, from *None of Us Will Return*. Reproduced by permission from Georges Borchardt, Inc., for Les Editions de Minuit.

Excerpt from *Into that Darkness: An Examination of Conscience* by Gitta Sereny. Copyright © 1974 by Gitta Sereny. Reproduced by permission from the Estate of Gitta Sereny and The Sayle Literary Agency.

"Forced March" by Miklós Radnóti, in *Forced March: Selected Poems*, translated by Clive Wilmer and George Gömöri. Copyright © 2003 by Enitharmon Press. Reproduced by permission from Enitharmon Press.

Excerpt from *Survival in Auschwitz* by Primo Levi, translated by Stuart Woolf. Reproduced by permission from Viking Books, Penguin Random House. Copyright © 1958 by Giulio Einaudi editore S.p.A.; translation copyright © 1959 by The Orion Press, Inc.

CPSIA information can be obtained
at www.ICGtesting.com
Printed in the USA
FSHW010928041218

9 781940 457239